THE
SEVEN DEADLY SINS
OF
Music Making

RICHARD FLOYD

THE
SEVEN DEADLY SINS
OF
Music Making

GIA Publications, Inc.
Chicago

The Seven Deadly Sins of Music Making
Richard Floyd

Layout and Design by Martha Chlipala
Edited by Bryan Gibson

G-10245
ISBN: 978-1-62277-448-7

Ashokan Farewell by Jay Ungar (pp. 64–67)
©1983 by Swinging Door Music.

Used with permission. All rights reserved.

TABLE OF
CONTENTS

PREFACE

So where was my head when I came up with the idea of writing a book on our musical transgressions? It was certainly not something that I was obsessing over. In fact, the thought of doing so had not remotely crossed my mind; that is, until Bruce Beach, past president of the Texas Bandmasters Association (TBA), asked me if I would consider presenting a clinic at the July 2015 Annual Convention.

It all started in January of that year while I was conducting a high school honor band in El Paso, Texas. Bruce had several students in the honor band, so there were several opportunities for the two of us to visit. At some point during the weekend he asked me if I would consider presenting a clinic session for the Texas Bandmasters Association gathering he was planning for the following summer. My first response to him was an attempt to deflect the request. I told Bruce I felt I had done so many clinics at TBA over the years that I was sure the band directors and other music educators had heard more than enough from me. He then asked if he might give me a call later in the month to talk more about it. I certainly agreed to the call, but I was secretly hoping he would get busy with his other presidential duties and the call would never come. It was not a matter of me being unwilling to speak but rather the notion on my part that all I had said over the years should suffice.

Sure enough a few weeks later the phone rang. It was Bruce. Soon the conversation turned to the subject of a potential clinic presentation. I continue to express reluctance but Bruce was very persuasive and unyielding in his desire to have me speak.

At some point I said, "Okay, I'll do it." His immediate response was, "Great! What are you going to talk about?" There was an extended silence on the phone as I pondered my response, and then without further hesitation I blurted out, "I think I'll do a clinic on the seven deadly sins of music making." He said, "Great!" He then thanked me and hung up.

For a very long time I sat at my desk staring out the window thinking, "What did I just get myself into?" I had no clue as to why that idea popped into my head or why I thought it might be a relevant topic. The conundrum plagued me for days as I attempted to assemble some focus for how I might proceed.

Not long afterwards I was visiting with my good friend James Keene, Professor Emeritus and retired director of bands at the University of Illinois. I shared my dilemma with him and ask for his thoughts. He immediately responded, "Dick, how in hell are you going to narrow it down to just seven?" The plot thickened!

The thought process continued. Then in the spring my wife Cheryl and I were returning to Austin after serving as evaluators at a music festival in Salt Lake City. On that flight everything began to take shape. I focused on the realization that we are all members of a passionate profession. We love what we do and how we do it. It would never be our deliberate intention to sin in our music making and teaching. So maybe our sins were not things that we did but rather things that we did not do. Perhaps they were sins of omission as opposed to sins of commission.

That assumption became the premise for my presentation. I developed an alpha version of the clinic to be delivered at the University of Texas Conducting Workshop in June and then refined the lecture for the Texas Bandmasters clinic the following month.

In most cases, that would have been the end of it. Mission accomplished! But as time went on I kept thinking there was much more to consider than I had been able to address in a one-hour clinic. The idea of a book surfaced, so here I am.

Let me quickly acknowledge my awareness that there is lots of subjectivity contained herein. I am fine with that. After all, the diversity of our opinions and points of view remains one of the joys of being music teachers and music makers. I can only submit to you that my message is steeped in my nearly six decades of engagement in our noble calling, enhanced by priceless interactions with some of the finest composers, conductors, and educators in our midst.

My challenge to you is to use my words as a springboard to reach your own conclusions as you refine and deepen your own personal world of artistry, all the while remembering that, in truth, the ultimate sin is to have no opinion or to make no judgments whatsoever.

ACKNOWLEDGMENTS

Writing a book is a lot of work. For me the process involved countless hours of thinking, reflecting, questioning, and then thinking some more. All this was intertwined with expansive periods of time staring at my computer, letting my fingers run rampant while questioning the worthiness of anything I might be attempting to say. Sometimes the words didn't come easily, and I struggled to bring clarity to what I was attempting to convey. Other times, the words leaped onto the computer screen with reckless abandon, giving me great personal satisfaction and a sense of accomplishment. Only to return the next day, read the same words again, and ask myself, "Dick, where was your head at when you thought this gibberish was remotely worthy of publication?"

Those were the times that I turned to friends, professional colleagues, and, of course, my amazing wife, Cheryl, for guidance and counsel. At the core of this abundant source of inspiration and support remain four of my dearest friends of over five decades. These kindred spirits are H. Robert Reynolds, Allan McMurray, Craig Kirchhoff, and Tom Lee. All are now retired from their own distinguished professorial collegiate careers. On more than one occasion I ran questions, thoughts, and book content by them for clarification, confirmation, or redirection. I always knew that what I would hear from them would be honest, candid, and steeped in their immeasurable artistry. I am so fortunate to have them as dear friends.

Also, a heartfelt thank you to Jerry Junkin, a dear friend and director of bands at the University of Texas. We have collaborated on so many levels for so many years. I cherish the amazing journey we continue to share. I have learned so much from him.

Another incomparable resource has been my many conversations with gifted composers who were so generous with their opinions, thoughts, and suggestions. Thank you to Frank Ticheli, John Mackey, Eric Whitacre, Mark Camphouse, and Brian Balmages for your wisdom and for sharing your abundant talent and knowledge.

Be assured that a critical necessity for the successful launch of a new book is the contributions of a highly skilled, collaborative editor. It was my good fortune to work with Bryan Gibson, Assistant Music Education Editor for GIA. His knowledge, insight, and impeccable attention to detail brought to my words an enhanced level of clarity and professionalism. I will remain eternally grateful for his astute advice and words of encouragement.

I remain eternally grateful to Dr. Cindy Houston, a former student, successful music educator, and longtime friend who generously created an abundance of musical excerpts intended to bring focus and clarity to many points discussed throughout the book. Cindy was there for me on my first book project, and I'm so thankful that she was willing to assist once again.

Then there is Cheryl, my wife and soul mate for over forty years. She patiently read every word of the manuscript again and again. Throughout the project she challenged me, encouraged me, and on some occasions even praised me. Whatever her response,

I knew it was delivered with love, honesty, and a shared passion for the professional world we both embrace. I will remain forever indebted to her for her incomparable encouragement and wise counsel throughout the project. Thank you, Cheryl!

WHAT ARE OUR SINS?

Music is never mere information.
— Bruce Adolphe[1]

So why begin a discourse on music making with a discussion of sin? On the surface it would appear difficult for one to draw any kind of correlation between our noble art of teaching and making music and the day-to-day human transgressions we refer to as being sinful. In truth, mankind seems to be preoccupied with sin. To make the point, the Merriam-Webster online dictionary suggests that this simple one-syllable word currently ranks in the top 30 percent of all word usage in the English language. Apparently, based on that statistical reality alone, the thought of sin is omnipresent, and the deed of sinning occupies a formidable place in our minds, our lives, and our conversations.

But what is a sin? What isn't a sin? Are there "big sins" as opposed to "little sins"? Are some sins more easily forgiven than others? This debate remains eternal and on one historical pathway can be traced back to the first biblical reference to the word found in the fourth chapter of Genesis where God states, "Sin lies at the door. And, its desire is for you, but you should rule over it."

But what exactly can and does that word mean? Once again returning to the well of knowledge found in the Merriam-Webster dictionary, we discover the word first means to be "an offense against religious or moral law." A second definition suggests "an action that is or is felt to be highly reprehensible." Yet a third definition is described as "an often-serious shortcoming or fault." Be prepared to hear a lot about this third definition as you read on.

Now, what about those "seven deadly sins" referenced in our book title? These cardinal sins can be traced back to the fourth century AD, so they have been with us for a very long time. For seventeen hundred years mankind has viewed the seven deadly sins to be those transgressions that are fatal to spiritual progress. They are also often referred to as the capital vices or cardinal sins. We know them today as:

LUST

GLUTTONY

GREED

SLOTH

WRATH

ENVY

PRIDE

Historians tell us the seven deadly sins have been a focal point of discussion and deliberation by scholars, authors, and theologians for centuries. Their severity and hierarchy have been debated in innumerable forums and discussed in depth through the ages. The French monk St. John Cassian (360–435 AD) went so far as to introduce the concept of an interconnected relationship between these sins. It was his belief that excesses in one vice would lead to other more severe vices—a slippery slope indeed!

By the fourteenth century public awareness of these capital vices or mortal sins had become so commonplace and ingrained in the human experience that we find them referenced countless times in the religion, literature, and art of Western culture. In addition, they, along with the Ten Commandments in the Bible, became the most popular and frequently used centerpieces for the discussion of ethics and the examination of conscience.

So, what does any of this philosophical and seemingly irrelevant discussion have to do with making music? For a moment let's consider that third definition of sin: "an often-serious shortcoming or fault." I would propose that in our desire to objectify every measurable aspect of music making we have created our own set of seven deadly sins. These sins, which I argue to be sins of omission as opposed to sins of commission, are a detriment to true musical progress. Equally, if not more important, committing one or more of these sins severely limits the scope of musical experiences we provide for our students.

Why? We obsess over every detail of notation that we view on a printed page of music. We study it, analyze it, strategize about how we will objectively teach it, and then we develop elaborate rubrics to critique and judge it. In the process, music unfortunately becomes an ink-on-paper, black-and-white quantitative issue that tends to be measured in pluses and minuses that are in no way representative of the true artistry of music making.

> Music cannot exist without notes and cannot live without expression.
>
> — David McGill in *Sound in Motion* (p. 264)

I attribute this fact to the absolute truth that nothing we see in terms of printed notation is actually music. Never forget that those spots on the page don't make any sound. In my mind, musical notation is "composer code." It doesn't become music until we "crack the code," solve the mystery, and bring the music to life. And, as is the case with most mysteries, the truth is rarely obvious or immediately accessed.

Look at it another way. In reality a score and set of parts is nothing more than a blueprint. A blueprint, in turn, is nothing more than an architect's functional two-dimensional rendering of his or her vision for the structure. Nothing on that blueprint defines the textures, hues, lighting, decor, or ambiance of the architectural space imagined. It's only after the plans are realized and then "humanized" does the true aesthetic human value of the edifice become a reality. Without that process of humanization, the building is nothing more than a set of functional walls and austere spaces.

Unfortunately, if we accept every aspect of musical notation literally, we run the risk of totally missing the essence of what the music is about or what the composer has to say. We may achieve the objective of being "correct," but in actuality that rarely translates into the ultimate vision for "making it right." The results, while being measurable, are sterile and lacking in those expressive, human qualities we refer to as artistry.

Let me put the difference between "correct" and "right" into context. A number of years ago I had the opportunity to work with a very wise gentleman by the name of Dr. Bill Stamps. He was a highly respected, successful school administrator and mentor to many. He often told the following story that clearly demonstrates the difference between being correct and being right.

A gentleman hailed a cab and gave the driver the address for his desired destination. The cabby dutifully transported the man as requested. Upon arrival the passenger asked the driver the amount of his fare. He was informed the fare was $16.35. The passenger promptly presented the driver a $10 bill, a $5 bill, a $1 bill, a quarter, and a dime. The cab driver counted and recounted the money, and with a raised eyebrow looked back over the seat at his passenger. The passenger in turn posed the question, "Isn't that correct?" The cab driver responded, "Yep, that is correct, but it sure as hell don't make it right."

What had the passenger failed to factor into this transaction? The gratuity, that something extra that would have brought gratitude and humanness to the transaction. We might even refer to it in our world of artistry as the "value added" that can only be achieved by going beyond the act of getting it "correct" and plumbing the depths of the intangible qualities that lie below the surface of the musical notation we see on the page.

By way of this preamble I would submit the following as our seven deadly sins of music making:

ARTICUALTION

DYNAMICS

RHYTHMS

TEMPO

LINE

SILENCE

PROPORTION

One can quickly conclude that there is nothing new, profound, or revealing here. After all, we would all agree that the first four of these seven elements of music making are dutifully addressed in our rehearsals on a routine basis. The quest for refinement within the context of these revered fundamentals is ingrained in our *modus operandi.* But do we sacrifice the more subjective, intangible components of music making in our effort to attain these objective, measurable goals?

Perhaps we can add a bit of clarity and specificity to our "deadly sins" by adding a few modifiers. How will our list look after doing so? The seven deadly sins of music making now read like this:

GENERIC ARTICULATION
UNCONVINCING DYNAMICS
PERCEIVING ALL RYHYTMS **LITERALLY**
BEING OBSESSED WITH TEMPO **MARKINGS**
ABSENCE OF LINE
IGNORING THE FUNCTION OF SILENCE **IN MUSIC**
FAILURE TO CONSIDER THE ROLE OF PROPORTION

It is my supposition that in our desire to master the technical essentials of our music we fail to embrace or give allegiance to the subtle, less palpable elements of music making that are the essence of artistic musical expression. We obsess over tone quality. We want all the notes to be correct. We monitor balance and blend. We fixate on the exactness of rhythms and embrace every symbol in the score and parts as being literal. To a point there is certainly nothing evil here as long as these objective elements of musical performance don't become an end unto themselves. If we do so, the concept of artistic expression is totally ignored. And remember, one definition of expression is "conveying of thoughts or feelings." Isn't that music making?

To put it another way, demonstrating how much you know is meaningless unless you also demonstrate and share with performers and listeners how much you feel.

Equally unfruitful is a strategy that embraces the notion that once all of the above are refined the music will "take care of itself." Concert violinist Ruth Waterman rebuts such a mindset in an article on her website entitled "Making Music: The Work of a Concert Violinist." She says:

> Despite the surprisingly widespread belief that all a player need do is to "play the notes", this very concept is nonsensical, for as soon as notes are sounded, they have a full complement of attributes: intensity, attack, dynamic level (loudness), warmth, character, direction, length, speed and so on. So if we assert that we are merely "letting the music play itself", it can only mean that we are forfeiting a conscious choice of attributes, allowing habitual, automatic ways of playing to overlay and strangle the voice of the composer.[2]

Perhaps with that compelling point of view in mind, a brief discussion of each of the aforementioned sins would give us a more contextual viewpoint of our deficiencies.

1. *Generic articulation.* If we are not careful, we will commit the sin of using articulation primarily to create precision and achieve what some refer to as (and I detest this term) "vertical alignment." Yet, in reality, the ultimate role of articulation is to create note shape and musical personality. It is our musical diction. Precision is a by-product.

2. *Unconvincing dynamics.* As we strive to refine balance, blend, and tuning, be aware of the sin of understating

dynamic contrasts. We are seduced into the practice of compressing dynamic range to such a degree that while the resulting sonority "sounds good" there is little or no perceived dynamic contrast. We have achieved one measurable objective but in doing so have sacrificed one of the most expressive elements of music making, dynamic contrast, in the process.

3. *Perceiving all rhythms literally.* As much as we would like to believe otherwise, musical rhythm is not finite. According to composer and conductor Bruno Walter, "the measurability of musical rhythm, and therefore the accurateness of its notation, is only approximate."[3] Divergence from the arithmetical exactness can and should occur, especially in the case of the short notes in dotted rhythms, which might be felt a little shorter and therefore placed a little later than prescribed by notation. Or perhaps a single note or small note grouping might be elongated to add nuance to a particular phrase or arrival point. If every beat, every measure, and every phrase is subjected to the unwavering, relentless throb of the metronome, the music remains mechanical and lifeless. It is a sin! What a shame.

4. *Being obsessed with tempo markings.* Certainly, tempo markings are there for a reason, and they offer valuable insight in terms of the composer's intent. There is no question that some must be precisely observed. But to embrace every metronome marking literally and precisely is a sin. There are countless factors that can influence tempo selection, including but not limited to the size of the ensemble, maturity of the musicians, and even the acoustics

of the performance space. Paul Hindemith perhaps said it best: "Don't play the tempo that is marked. Play the tempo that is right!" More about that later.

5. *Absence of line.* Never forget, music travels linearly. It tells a story, explores emotions, and takes the musician and the listener on a journey. In reality it is a sin to obsess over the vertical factors and objective content of the music to the extent that there is little or no consideration given to how the music unfolds from note to note, from measure to measure, from phrase to phrase, or from beginning to end. Without line music becomes an endless sequence of notes and rhythms that are void of relationships and meaningful connections.

6. *Ignoring the function of silence in music.* Silence is a priceless quality. Leopold Stokowski proclaimed that silence is the canvas upon which we paint our music. It is an integral component of music making. How long should it last? Is it passive or does it contain quiet energy? How does the music emerge from the silence and then return to the silence? To fail to consider these limitless options is a sin.

7. *Failure to consider the role of proportion.* Proportion is an essential component in all of the arts. Once again, in our desire to "get it right" we fail to consider the relationships between dynamics, tempos, note lengths, and articulations.

    We commit the sin of being confined and limited by the notes on the printed page. According to Pablo Casals, "The written note is like a strait-jacket, whereas music, like life itself, is constant movement, continuous spontaneity, free from any restriction."[4] He went on to say, "There are so many excellent instrumentalists who are completely obsessed by the printed note, whereas it has a very limited power to express what the music actually means."[5]

Now, with all that said, be assured there is a place in all of our rehearsals for objectivity and measurable outcomes. That is the craft of what we do. But as in so much of life, remember all things in moderation. On occasion let your heart and your musical soul guide your rehearsal. Take time to enjoy the art of your music as opposed to the craft of your music. In the words of Saint Francis of Assisi:

He who works with his hands is a laborer.
He who works with his hands and his head is a craftsman.
He who works with his hands and his head and
his heart is an artist.

Which are you? Are you a laborer, a craftsman, or an artist? Which do you want to be? The chapters to follow are intended to guide you on your journey to a world of artistic, expressive music making that goes beyond the printed page.

CHAPTER I

SIN #1: GENERIC ARTICULATION

It's a wonderful thing—every note must have life!
— Pablo Casals[6]

L et's begin with the postulate that articulation be viewed as a fundamental musical parameter that determines how a single note or series of notes might be sounded. Articulation defines not only the beginning and end of a note but also the shape of the note and the qualities of attack and decay. There is also the potential for articulation to modify timbre, dynamics, and pitch.

With that said, if you ask a group of students, or directors for that matter, what word pops into their mind when they hear the term "articulation," inevitably the almost universal response will be tonguing. Certainly, at least in the case of wind instruments, tonguing is an integral component of many styles of articulation, but it plays a minimal or only subtle role in others. Yet universally in the wind instrument world the tongue is viewed to be closely associated with all things articulation.

Consider why that might be. It has been my observation that the sin of generic articulation oftentimes stems from the erroneous point of view in the mind of many directors that the primary function of articulation is to create precision via tonguing. In other words, articulation is the mechanical goal of attacking notes together and then releasing notes together with the intent of achieving what some refer to as "vertical alignment." If all members of the ensemble start and stop together with uniformity and clarity, the mission is accomplished. All true, if ensemble exactness is the sole desired outcome. It is an objective, observable, and measurable goal, but it is generally void of any qualities of nuance, style, contour, interpretation, expressiveness, or (here again is that word I keep coming back to) artistry.

I am also of the notion that we as conductors/educators should be mindful of the potential liability associated with the frequent use of the word "attack." Why? If you look at the definition of the word "attack" you will see no reference to its application in music making. Instead you will see phrases such as "harm using violence," "infect somebody or damage something," "to act violently against someone or something," and so on. Yet it is a word that we freely associate with all things articulation. I get that the word "attack" is in our musical lexicon, but that doesn't make it any more palatable to my taste. Certainly, it is nothing more or less than a mindset, but I prefer to seek kinder, gentler, concise descriptors that are more closely associated with the human experience of making music.

So, for the sake of our discussion let's take a more inclusive, artistic stance. Let's think of articulation as being musical, expressive diction, if you will. To make the point, look at multiple definitions of the word "diction" as opposed to the definitions of the word "attack" just referenced and you will see reoccurring references to terms like "enunciation," "expression," "inflection," and the selection of more subtle words to convey a mood, tone, or atmosphere. Sounds like expressive music making to me! I like to think of articulation as a primary element that gives each note meaning, personality, and context. Notice I said every note, not just some of the notes. Certainly, all notes are not created equal, and some notes are more important and communicative than others, but I have concluded that all notes must have life and a compelling reason for being.

Interestingly, in his book *The Art of Musicianship*, French horn artist and teacher Philip Farkas expresses his belief that in music the words "articulate" or "articulation" refer to the combination of slurs and attacks found in the music. He proposes that the term not be limited to the physical act of starting or stopping a single note in some fashion with the tongue, but rather the broader spectrum of a combination of attacks, releases, and slurs used in concert to create expressive musical communication. It is the way that notes interact, relate, and create meaning. I could not agree more.

> Three features of articulation are of particular interest to performing musicians: 1. the constant reference to articulation as being part of human speech; 2. the connecting, uniting or joining together of the various parts of speech to form a complete idea; 3. the act of pronouncing clearly and distinctly.
>
> — Philip Farkas in *The Art of Musicianship* (p. 28)

Consider the more traditional articulation markings we are accustomed to seeing.

none   tenuto   staccato   accent   marcato

Each one of us can submit a generic definition of what each marking might approximate. Furthermore, an excursion on the Internet will reveal a plethora of interpretive options. But "bumper sticker" descriptions tell us little or nothing about the contextual application of these markings in a specific piece, musical genre, or the output of a specific composer. The bottom line: To a large degree these markings are meaningless without context. The composer, the style of the music, the original source of the musical content, the musical period represented, and the musical intent are among many factors that all have a bearing on the desired result for any articulation marking. In truth, the options in terms of how a particular articulation marking might be interpreted are limitless. One might argue that we could have an infinite array of markings for articulation and there would still be room for yet more variables and expressive interpretive judgments. It is our artistic musical intuitiveness that must ascertain the subtle expressiveness in the music and then bring it to life.

So, let's consider other descriptors that might be more closely associated with articulation that go beyond the simple physical act of tonguing. What if our approach to articulation was driven by other observable properties? Consider such factors as:

- Length
- Weight
- Style
- Mood
- Context
- Personality
- Composer
- Musical period
- Original musical source (e.g., orchestral transcription, choral music text, jazz, other)

With thoughtful reflection, you might want to add some descriptors of your own. After all, that is one of the beauties of music making. There can be countless satisfying answers and we each have the opportunity to put our own personal musical thumbprint on the musical outcome. How exciting!

Now, as you do so a whole new palette of expressive, musical, and artistic outcomes is introduced. Precision, while always important, is no longer core to our commitment to expressive articulation. It is the art, not the craft, that truly matters. At this point, articulation no longer simply refers to the physical act of tonguing on a wind instrument, bowing on a string instrument, or striking a percussion instrument, but the expressive, emotional, artistic content that is the desired end result.

If you accept this premise, then you will likely agree that the role of articulation in music should be to communicate a feeling and/or emotion as opposed to simply starting and stopping a note together with some generic inference to a musical style. The possibility now exists to use articulation in an artistic milieu that embraces note shape, personality, expressiveness, and interpretive nuance. The challenge then becomes guiding students to understand how the physical attributes of articulation can function in concert to create a broad array of note shapes that are not only precise, but also, and more important, musically expressive. In my previous book, *The Artistry of Teaching and Making Music,* the sixth chapter goes into great detail about how to achieve uniformity of articulation with an emphasis on creating a vocabulary of note shape, nuance, and expressiveness. My intent here is not to restate those fundamental concepts but rather to explore the artistic application of various styles of articulation.

There's a lot to discuss here.

NOTES VOID OF ARTICULATION MARKINGS

So, let's begins with a series of quarter notes void of any articulation marking whatsoever. What to do? Does one arbitrarily decide that these notes are to be played non-expressive and void of musical personality? Obviously one approach can simply be to use a generic, connected style of articulation that identifies the notes and rhythm as a row of quarter notes void of emotion or personality. Certainly, that would not be wrong.

But is that enough? Surely there should be some consideration of context or musical intent. There must be more than the notation that appears on the page. Does the score suggest a particular mood or expressive style? Is there "hidden meaning" to be discovered and revealed? Can articulation be used to communicate that? Perhaps there should be a little more weight on the beginning of each note intended to add drama and a sense of urgency to the line. Maybe the articulation should be slightly blurred to create a more mysterious, subdued interpretation. If there is melodic percussion in play, perhaps a slightly firmer stick selection might be used to subtly define the beginning of each note. Above all, embrace the axiom that absence of articulation markings does not imply absence of musical style.

What if these notes are embedded in the trio strain of a march that is sounded the first time *pianissimo* and on the repeat *fortissimo*? With no articulation markings, would the articulation be the same both times? It could be, based on the absence of any markings. But what would be the musical outcome if on the first time through at the *pianissimo* marking the notes were played as smooth as possible with only a subtle but defined legato articulation, and then on the repeat at full volume the notes were played slightly detached and with a heavier "front end" on each note, in a more marcato style? The contrast would be musically compelling, and the sense of finality to the final strain would be significantly more engaging for the performers and the audience. Is that *the* right way? Not necessarily. There could easily be other options to contemplate. Other interpretations could be equally compelling. The only necessity is to have an interpretive point of view that goes beyond the shorthand on the printed page that we refer to as musical notation.

Then, on the other hand, perhaps the absence of any implied style can be viewed as musically appropriate and even essential. I'm thinking here of examples such as the dramatic metamorphous that begins at measure 281 in Frank Ticheli's *Angels in the Architecture*. It starts with a small assembly of low woodwinds and horns with support from string bass and timpani. The instrumentation grows without a single articulation marking for some thirty-five measures. It is my belief that this austere ninety-second musical journey should be void of any articulation style beyond what is required to define the rhythmic outline of the lines, with the string bass and timpani reinforcing the "heartbeat" of the music. The descriptive word that comes to my mind is "throbbing." The ultimate goal is to prepare the listener for the vivid drama and the impactful moment that evolves as the dynamics grow and the presence of accents begins to emerge. In this case, a placid, pale style of articulation is a good thing and serves a very compelling musical function, as it veils the impactful moments to come.

The challenge is clear. Even notation void of any indication of articulation must be approached musically and with a commitment to expressive music making.

Now let's discuss some of the more common articulation markings in no particular order.

TENUTO

Consider the marking we commonly refer to as "tenuto" or sometimes "sostenuto." There is general agreement that this marking can mean either to hold the note in question its full length (in some cases slightly longer) and/or play the note with a bit more emphasis, stress, volume, weight, or resonance. In either case the net result is to create a human connection with that note or notes. Once again questions arise since there are multiple ways to approach notes with this marking, and as always it is the context of the music that guides the approach. The end result between the performer and listener should be a shared experience that can be either unexpected or, in other cases, anticipated. Sometimes I refer to notes and passages with this marking to be like a firm handshake.

Let's look at some examples.

In *Sheltering Sky*, John Mackey uses the tenuto marking to call attention to certain notes that he wants to stress with firmness. He also includes the words "a tempo, but very freely" at Letter A. It is my view that there is license here to slightly stretch the tempo around these tenuto notes while giving a slight amount of stress to emphasize their importance, the goal being to shine an audible spotlight on the role these specific notes play in the melodic content and in the harmonic architecture of the music. The result is compelling, provided that it is organic as opposed to an arbitrary, mechanical exertion of pressure on a single note.

Sheltering Sky

An example of where this marking plays a totally different role occurs at measure 41 in *Shenandoah* by Frank Ticheli. At this point in the work the timeless melody is being masterfully stated by a flute trio as a three-part canon while being underscored in augmentation by the clarinets. Here the tenuto marking is used to emphasize the restatement of pivotal notes in the melody. Any elongation of these notes would easily erode the musical momentum that is unfolding. All that is needed is a slight increase in volume, stress, weight, or intensity to emphasize the interplay of the intertwined melody in triplicate. The "heartbeat" of the music should remain steady and flowing forward. The result might be viewed as an "echo effect."

Shenandoah, mm. 41–46

Another consideration might be to contemplate what other elements are present in the score. For example, in *Lullaby to the Moon* by Brian Balmages, at measure 41 the composer inserts tenuto markings on multiple notes in the wind instrument lines. Taken at face value it would be possible to conclude that it could be musically effective, and appropriate for that matter, to stretch those beats to create drama as the musical journey builds to the climactic G minor chord in measure 57. However, looking further down the score will reveal that there are moving eighth notes and quarter note triplets in the melodic percussion parts. These rhythmic moving lines would suggest that these tenuto markings must be interpreted as stress points with audible enhanced intensity pressing on the notes but with no lengthening of note value that would cloud the interplay between the winds and the underlying "motor" in the melodic percussion. It is worthy to note that with further score study one discovers this is the only place in the entire piece that the tenuto marking is used. That fact alone suggests that these notes must mean something.

Lullaby to the Moon, mm. 41–43

So, when might it be musically appropriate to slightly lengthen notes marked tenuto? Look at the woodwind line beginning in measure 112 in Alfred Reed's transcription of the *La Procession du Rocio* by Joaquín Turina. Reed has assigned an articulation marking to virtually every note in the phrase, culminating with a tenuto marking on the downbeat of measure 114 that introduces the oboe solo. To my ear this transition of music styles transcends tempo and begs for the tenuto quarter note on beat one to be slightly extended to create a more musical bond with the oboe solo that is to follow.

La Procession du Rocio, mm. 112–114

Now look at the transition into Letter T in the same work. Here most of the winds have eighth notes, leading to triplets that transition into a tempo change to Andante con moto at Letter T. All notes are marked tenuto. If one simply adds weight to each of those notes, the overall musical effect is redundant. Each note is more of the same and the tenuto loses its effectiveness. But what if that stress is combined with a gradual broadening of the pulse that foreshadows the tempo change that is looming in the next measure? The result can be a seamless, expressive transition that is proportional and musically appropriate for the drama that is to follow. (Proportion is another sin that we will visit later.)

La Procession du Rocio

Yes, there is a red flag here. In a conversation with composer Eric Whitacre, he stated:

> My general feeling with articulations, especially the tenuto marking, is that conductors misuse them. Or rather, they don't make them musical; they just lean on the notes. So, the overall phrase doesn't sound natural at all. It sounds like a machine reproducing the concept of a musical line. It is all brain and no heart.

He went on to say, "For a good conductor the harmonic language (plus the inherent musical line and architecture) make it obvious where the tenuto should go." Well said! (More about line in a later chapter.)

STACCATO

People who think of the word "tonguing" when they hear the word "articulation" similarly tend to associate the word "short" with all things staccato. But once again there is a fallacy here. In the original Italian the word means "detached" or "disconnected." There is no reference simply to the adjective "short" or the relative shape of the front end of the note. To complicate the issue is the reality that the application of the staccato style of articulation can produce very different results depending on the instrument being played. For example, a violinist using a rapid sequence of fast martelé strokes in the same direction to achieve a staccato style will hear a very different acoustical result from what one would expect to hear when staccato is played on an oboe or large brass wind instrument. Consequently, we enter this particular discussion with a broad range of variables already at play.

Perhaps a point of departure might be to consider adjectives other than "short" that could be used to frame the role of the staccato marking in our world of music making. Depending on the music before us, one or more of the following words might be relevant.

- Light
- Crisp
- Buoyant
- Sharp
- Brittle
- Resonate
- Bubbly
- Effervescent
- Dry

What would we conclude if we took any of these adjectives and associated them to a compositional style or even a specific composer? Examine the following two excerpts from Persichetti's *Symphony for Band*. In both cases the articulation marking is a simple staccato marking, but I would argue the desired musical outcome is totally different.

At the end of the third movement, I view the two repeated eighth notes played by the woodwinds and low brass to be a final "tip of the hat" to the dance-like B theme of the movement. The first time this music appears it is accompanied with the musical term *giocoso*, meaning to perform in a happy, merry, playful manner. If this is a musically valid point of view, would adjectives such as "sharp," "brittle," or "crisp" come to mind, or would the musical intent be better served by referencing such descriptors as "light," "buoyant," or even "humorous"? These notes might even be slightly lifted.

Symphony for Band, **Mvt. III**

Continuing into the fourth movement one immediately encounters the identical staccato marking but in a totally different context. Is this music to remain light and buoyant? I think not. "Crisp," "sharp," or "brittle" would be more applicable.

Symphony for Band, Mvt. IV, mm. 1–4

But what if we were making an artistic decision about the stunning last three notes of the second movement of Ingolf Dahl's *Sinfonietta*? Crisp, sharp, or brittle would be far removed from our interpretative contemplation. Look at what is going on here. There is glockenspiel, xylophone, and triangle in play in the percussion. Reinforcing the final major third there is a pizzicato string base tonic concert D-flat. Between the melodic percussion and the pizzicato string bass there are compelling clues as to the note length and style of the staccato in the wind instruments. Immediately the words "resonate," "light," or perhaps "buoyant" come to mind.

Sinfonietta, Mvt. II, mm. 120–121

Speaking of the pizzicato string bass, more often than not its presence can be a bellwether in terms of defining uniform note length and style, particularly when doubled with low reeds and/or low brass. Such scoring occurs on multiple occasions in *Children's*

March: "Over the Hills and Far Away" by Percy Grainger, edited by Mark Rogers. The eight-measure phrase beginning at measure 53 is a prime example. To my ear the default note shape and length for all instruments should be the pizzicato bass.

Children's March, mm. 53–54

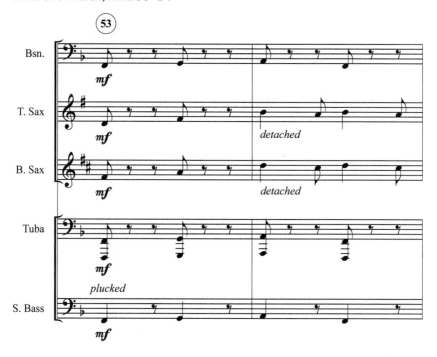

Grainger's scoring features a lush woodwind choir of resonate reed instruments reinforced by tuba and string bass. The string bass in Grainger's words is "plucked." Unfortunately, many wind instrument players will focus on the shortness of the notes, clip the note length, and leave the tones dry and lacking in resonance. On the other hand, if all players bond with the sound of the double bass and match that front end and note length, the result will be a bass line that has enough roundness and warmth to underscore the harmonic content that is unfolding in other instruments.

Pedagogically, another way to think of it is for the wind instruments to blow *through* these notes as opposed to blowing *at* them.

ACCENT

Now behold the enigmatic marking that is often denoted simply as "an accent." In truth we really have no agreement as to a definitive name for this marking. In some reference resources it is referred to as an "accent," while others associate it with the term "marcato." For the purposes of our discussion I will use the word "accent" and save the term "marcato" for that marking that sometimes is affectionately referred to as a "housetop accent." More about that marking later.

So, if we can't come to a consensus on what it is called, how in the world are we going to know what to do with it? I would submit that there are three observable qualities that might be present. First, to some degree there will be a percussive quality associated with the front end of the note. Secondly, in most cases, but not all, repeated accented notes will not touch each other. There will be a slight separation helping to define the front end of each accent. Finally, there will often be a slight increase of volume on accented notes, to what degree and with what frequency will depend on the context of the music at hand.

Beyond those three traits we are once again in a world of subjectivity guided by our musical intuitiveness. Conversely, it is important to note that you rarely see this marking in sustained, lyrical, chorale-like music. It simply is not a part of that musical palette.

So, let's start with a discussion of words that begin with consonants. These words require some use of the tongue or lips to launch them. Consider the following examples:

- Ball
- Bat
- Bite
- Dig
- Dog
- Dot
- Jerk
- Pool
- Tah
- Tee
- Zing

While each of the words referenced has its own persona, they collectively share in common some degree of impactful, percussive beginning. In some cases, the beginning is abrupt and explosive while in others it is subtle, faint, and almost inaudible. But in every case, there is a defined front end to the word. There can also be a variation in volume as mentioned above. Words like "pool" or "ball" seem to call for very little dynamic inflection, while words like "dot," "zing," or "jerk" tend to be spoken with noticeable zest or gusto. From my point of view, this analogy vividly reveals the limitless spectrum of options we have at our disposal to expressively interpret notes calling for an accent.

Our repertoire is filled with boundless examples of the diversity associated with this articulation marking.

Look at *Scenes from "The Louvre"* by Norman Dello Joio. There is a glorious moment near the end of the first movement at measure 41 where multiple accents are used to add impact to the end of the movement. (Let's use the trumpet lines for our example.) How best to achieve the desired musical result? The ensemble is in full force and the dynamic volume has been established as *fortissimo sempre.* Thus, more volume is probably not the answer. Based on these parameters, I would propose that the accent could be best achieved with a slight separation and a bit more front end on the accented notes that calls attention to their significance and is in distinct contrast with the music just heard. There is a fanfare quality suggested here as well.

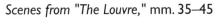

Scenes from "The Louvre," mm. 35–45

Also consider the reality that composers routinely use the accent mark to imply countless different subtle nuances of musical expressiveness within their own body of work. Take the following two excerpts from music by Frank Ticheli.

The first example appears in measures 60–63 of *Shenandoah.* The music is broad and full of grandeur. I would argue that these accents must be approached with elegant strength and power and essentially void of any percussiveness. Descriptors that come to mind are "regal," "grand," or "stately." Even a sense of reverence might be appropriate. The air rather than the tongue should do most of the work here.

(Note: I consistently minimize using words that might be viewed as technical descriptors and instead gravitate to words that are more closely associated with human emotions and experiences. After all, that is where the real music lives.)

Shenandoah, mm. 60–63

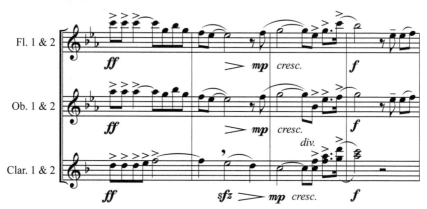

Now let's compare that to a brief woodwind excerpt from *Blue Shades*. In measures 90–94 we see the identical marking in the flute and clarinet lines. But here the role is totally different. The music is jazzy and full of panache as it drives toward an arrival point in measure 95. These accents beg for lots of bite, front end, and slight separation. Perhaps there should be a feeling of reckless abandon. Just go for it! The style called for in the *Shenandoah* excerpt would be totally inappropriate and would actually distract from the musical personality of the moment.

Blue Shades, mm. 90–94

Finally let's examine two examples in the first movement of *Prelude, Siciliano and Rondo* by Malcolm Arnold, arranged by John Paynter. The opening carries a certain quality of majesty, perhaps regal in style. I do not view these accents as being percussive and impactful or executed with a lot of front end on the notes. Rather, the musically appropriate result might best be achieved simply by utilizing a slightly crisper articulation combined with more air infused into the beginning of each accented note.

Prelude, Siciliano and Rondo, mm. 1–3

Now let's fast-forward to Letter A and the preceding measure. Again, accents are called for but in a totally different context. The accented, descending eighth note line in the lower voices crescendos to set up the fanfare-like motive stated by the cornets and horns at Letter A. These notes require a more aggressive stance. I would even argue that you could gradually intensify the accents as the A-flat major scale descends, so as the volume increases the accents become more pronounced. This interpretation beautifully sets up the fanfare quality of the motive stated by cornet and horns in the next measure that, to my ear, calls for a bit more breadth and bravura in the musical style.

Prelude, Siciliano and Rondo

So, within a matter of nine measures and some twenty seconds of music, the perplexing simple accent mark affords us the opportunity to consider three distinctly unique musical styles all under the broad heading of accents. The bottom line: There is no *one right way* to play accents, and contemplating these kinds of informed musical judgments is one of the most joyful aspects of making music. Our greatest sin is to make no judgments at all and simply let the music "play itself."

MARCATO

Finally, we have the marcato accent marking, often referred to by the colloquial term "housetop accent." Keep in mind that the term "marcato" in Italian is defined as "well marked." Following our previous tack, let's consider words that help define the musical application of this term.

- Distinct
- Firm
- Forceful
- Hard
- Marked
- Percussive
- Pronounced
- Robust
- Separated
- Strong
- Violent (sometimes)

You get the idea. One might also consider notes marked marcato to be played in some form or fashion of an accented staccato.

While there remains a broad range of options all under the heading of interpretation, I would submit that the marcato marking is the most narrowly defined style of articulation. The marcato style is going to have clearly audible weight, firmness, volume, and separation, resulting in a distinctive contrast to all other articulation markings. Marcato notes do not touch their neighbors. They "mean business"!

There is yet another red flag here. One might argue that the marcato style is the most "physical" style of traditional articulation.

The attack is forceful and generally there is a detectable increase in volume. The potential exists for an overly percussive, unmusical attack, and/or a distorted, strident tone quality. This outcome is especially true with younger or less mature players. It thus remains the role of the teacher/conductor to be vigilant in ensuring that, regardless of the aggressiveness of the marcato style, the overriding priority always remains beautiful, focused, and undistorted tone quality.

HYBRID ARTICULATIONS

Of course, there can be limitless combinations of articulation markings, and many contemporary composers have created hybrid indications of a specific style they are seeking. For example, in the music of composers such as Omar Thomas, Frank Ticheli, David Biedenbender, and John Mackey, you will see various combinations of tenuto, staccato, accent, and marcato. The challenge then is to come to some artistic decision about how these hybrid markings should be interpreted. I submit that there are two primary reference sources for doing so.

The first is composer intent. In order to arrive at a determination about what the composer is seeking, one must look at the composer's body of work, not just a single score. Becoming familiar with a composer's personal language and compositional style will reveal much about what they hope to hear when they indicate a hybrid articulation marking.

Secondly, there must be some consideration of musical context. The overall style and mood of the music reveals much about how one might interpret these distinctive notations. The beauty is that there exists the possibility for more than one right answer. All we can expect is that our interpretation is driven by thoughtful contemplation and not merely a "guess."

In summary, articulation markings might be best considered as "musical guideposts." Their role is to give us an artistic reference point regarding the composer's intent. They should not be viewed as being literal or finite. Nor can we assign hard-and-fast rules to their application. Above all, they are not intended to or capable of placing us in the center of the musical bull's-eye. As conductor/teachers that is what we do, and that's where the fun comes in.

Chapter 2

SIN #2: UNCONVINCING DYNAMICS

The dynamics never sit. They are always in motion.
— Robert Shaw

L et's begin this discussion with a simple premise. In the world of music performance, dynamics are totally valueless. Dynamic contrasts are void of meaning. They are simply of no consequence; that is, until the dynamics are perceived by the listener. One can contemplate dynamics, ponder their role in music, and then attempt to infuse audible contrasts into the sonic milieu. But if the end result is not perceived by the listener, does not connect with the members of the audience, does not intensify the message of the music, then for all intents and purposes the dynamics simply don't exist and are of no meaningful consequence.

Look at it from a composer's point of view. In April 1806 Beethoven wrote to opera singer and stage director Sebastian Mayer:

Please request Herr v. Seyfried to conduct my opera to-day; I myself want today to see and hear it at a distance; by that means, at any rate, my patience will not be so severely tried, as when close by I hear my music murdered. I cannot help thinking that it is done purposely. I say nothing about the wind instruments, but that all *pp*, *crescendos*, all *decrescendos* and all *fortes ff* were struck out of my opera; no notice is taken of a single one. If that's what I have to hear, there is no inducement to write anything more!

Your friend,
Beethoven[7]

Dynamics clearly mattered to Beethoven. Basically, to me, he is saying here that if he had to listen to his music with no dynamic contrast then there was really no reason for him to continue composing. There is a powerful message here. It is clear that he felt that dynamics were a fundamental "lifeblood" of his music and our art, I might add. After all, the presence of dynamics is intimately intertwined into so much that we hold dear in the art of music making. It is central to an expansive spectrum of musical expression. The beauty and flow of a musical line without the presence of dynamics is difficult, if not impossible, to imagine. Dynamics add contrast to repeated melodic material. They give anticipation to what is yet to come, bring highlight to expressive points of arrival, and create reflection on what has just transpired. A compelling *forte-piano* is impossible without the audible infusion of abrupt dynamic contrast. The musical gesture we refer to as *niente* is simply unattainable without the subtle infusion of waning dynamics. What is sometimes referred to as "expressive inflection" simply cannot occur without the use of dynamic contrast. The list goes on.

[Dynamics] are one of the composer's most basic tools with which to color, to decorate the music, to delineate form and structure, to clarify lines and layers of music, to create variety of expression—in short, to create real music.

— Gunther Schuller in
    *The Compleat
    Conductor* (p. viii)

Yet, with all this compelling evidence to the contrary, it has been my observation that we as conductor/educators yield to the temptation to marginalize and subdue dynamics in an effort to "sound good." We sacrifice volume and intensity (more about intensity later) to ensure that the overall sonority is balanced, blended, and in tune. At the other end of the dynamic spectrum, we are cautious not to play "too soft" for fear that the tone quality will become fuzzy, weak, and/or unfocused. We want our music making to be orderly, perhaps a bit controlled. As we proceed down the slippery slope of "playing it safe" we soon find ourselves in what I sometimes refer to as the "*mf* world." The bland end result is never too loud or too soft but always safe, essentially being void of expressiveness and artistry.

A music performance in this compressed dynamic range might be viewed as analogous with eating all foods at a lukewarm temperature or with neutral seasonings. The nutrients are certainly ingested, but the aesthetic of fine dining is simply non-existent. Equally unfulfilling would be a lecture given in a non-expressive monotone. The words might be present but hollow and void of intellectual content or emotional messaging.

From the first time I read the words of Pablo Casals, I have been inspired and challenged by them: "Remember that all music, in general, is a succession of rainbows."[8] That revelation was life changing. The year was 1983. For me personally it was a "eureka" moment I have never forgotten. What a beautiful thought. What are the elements of a rainbow? What we observe in–this artful handiwork of nature is a breathtaking blend of beautiful shape and captivating color. Think how effectively the infusion of this imagery into our music making could enhance the beauty of our efforts. The result can be a compelling auditory sensation of shape and color created through the artistic contemplation and application of dynamic contrast. To this day there is never a rehearsal or a performance in which Casal's eloquent words are not resonating in my musical soul.

Consider the proposition that we, as music makers, are in the business of what I often refer to as "artful exaggeration." Nowhere is this reckoning more important or critical than in our consideration of dynamics. One must determine the sonic landscape of the music at hand and then establish a dynamic palette that communicates to the listener the expressive qualities the music has to offer. Let me reiterate: It is the dynamic contrast we communicate to the listener, not the dynamic contrast we hear in our head or on the podium.

Yet in reality it is commonplace to hear simple melodies and repeated motives played precisely and accurately but void of any dynamic interest. Doing so is safe, inoffensive, and without artistic risk—in a word, boring!

So, after that extended preamble, what are our options? Let's begin with the obvious: the use of immediately contrasting dynamic volumes, a technique often referred to as terraced dynamics. This distinctive technique was a frequently heard performance practice in the music of the Renaissance and early Baroque period. In some settings it remains an effective, viable option today. There is nothing subtle here. The strategy is simply to play some phrases loud and some phrases soft.

Let's use the nostalgic, timeless melody "Long, Long Ago," written in 1833 by the English composer Thomas Haynes Bayly to explore this concept. The melody is primarily scale-wise and there are essentially only two rhythmic motives. Certainly, it can be performed at a single, moderate dynamic with satisfying results. Its compelling simplicity will be clearly apparent and recognized by the listener. It goes like this.

Long, Long Ago Excerpt #1

But what if contrasting dynamics were utilized to add interest? Nothing fancy. No crescendos or diminuendos. Simple contrasting phrases played loud or soft will do. The result is a satisfying example of terraced dynamics.

Long, Long Ago Excerpt #2

Another option might be:

Long, Long Ago Excerpt #3

You get the idea. There are myriad possibilities, with each option adding its own spin to the melodic content. Do not forget every one of these dynamic options is accessible to a young musician once they have mastered the notes and rhythms. This is not "advanced artistry" by any means.

In the final analysis, our musical world has thus expanded and the artistic intent (I love that term) of our music making is elevated. And it is probably worth stating here that the addition of dynamics is fulfilling both for the performer and the listener. It is more satisfying for all parties. It is very much like a conversation—a dialogue that is infused with personality and meaning, enlivened by the rise and fall of dynamic inflection.

The next step might be to use dynamics to enhance musical line and phrasing. Can we agree that a melodic line accurately performed in terms of notes, rhythms, tone quality, and intonation but lacking dynamic contrast is lifeless? It's very much like citing the Pledge of Allegiance or The Lord's Prayer in a monotone. There is no aesthetic, expression, or inflection. (More about inflection later.) It is the infusion of dynamics that brings the musical line to life. The rise, fall, and pacing of the dynamics breathes life and artistry into the notes.

But what is the proper application of dynamics to achieve a satisfying musical phrase? Is there a formula that guarantees a musical result? Far from it! I will say it again: This is one of the beauties of music. There are boundless options for capturing what Leopold Mozart referred to as "light and shade." Once again, the only sin we can commit here is the sin of omission; that is, to make no judgment whatsoever and thus allowing the "musical chips" to fall where they may.

Let's see how this might apply to the beautiful *Ashokan Farewell* by Jay Ungar. This haunting melody was composed as a part of the soundtrack for Ken Burns's television documentary *The Civil War*. A quick visit to YouTube will reveal countless versions of this melancholy melody by such musical artists as James Galloway, Mark O'Connor, and the Osborne Brothers. It transcends genres.

> Every care must be taken to find and to render the affect which the composer wished to have brought out. . . . Indeed, one must know how to change from soft to loud without directions and of one's own accord, each at the right time; for this, in the familiar language of painters, means light and shade.
>
> — Leopold Mozart, as quoted in David Blum's *Casals and the Art of Interpretation* (p. 17)

Ashokan Farewell **Excerpt #1**

What we see in this excerpt is a simple sixteen-measure structure of unadorned notes and rhythms. It represents only a fragment of the entire song. There is nothing more and nothing

In silent score study it is so easy to focus on the objective notes and rhythms with little or no awareness of dynamic nuance. Strive to refine the practice of "hearing dynamics in your mind's ear" as you visually ponder the notes and rhythms on the page.

less. Sitting silently on the page it is soundless. Consider it as raw material ready to be transformed into a thing of tender beauty.

So, let's get started. Hear the melody in your head or, better yet, sing it or play it on an instrument. Compelling, isn't it? But what is missing? At this point there is no artistry, humanness, or personality, if you will. They are simply cold, expressionless notes.

Now as you hear the melody, begin to think about the dynamic palette that you have as an expressive resource. What is possible in terms of infusing expressive dynamic qualities into the theme? There is no limit to the options.

What if we applied Casals's belief that "all music, in general, is a succession of rainbows"? We would play the anacrusis very softly, setting the stage for a gradual crescendo that culminates on the A in measure 8. There would be a strong sense of arrival at the dominant. At that point the dynamics begin a return to an approximation of the beginning dynamic in measure 16. All of a sudden, each note has purpose and direction, thus creating a musical architecture that transcends the notation. It would sound like this.

Ashokan Farewell Excerpt #2

There also could be rainbows within rainbows, thus creating cascading sub-phrases that intertwine with one another such as:

Ashokan Farewell Excerpt #3

All good but many more options remain. The stage is now set for an abundance of variables in the application of dynamics to create more subtle and nuanced interpretations of the melodic content. Perhaps the opening four measures could be simply stated in a soft, reflective mood, then a more abrupt crescendo leads the listener to the midpoint of the phrase, followed by sudden contrasts in dynamics from *subito piano* to *subito forte* and a culminating four-measure diminuendo leading to the cadence. This interpretation might look something like this:

Ashokan Farewell **Excerpt #4**

Yet another interpretation might be to lead the listener on a roller coaster of dynamics embedded with subtle surprises, setting up a strong sense of arrival on the final four measures:

Ashokan Farewell Excerpt #5

We could easily continue this exercise with innumerable variations. Are some interpretations better or more satisfying than others? Perhaps. But the quest for artistry involves risks and the application of creative thinking. There is an important caveat here: There is no need, and arguably it is counterproductive, to wait for technical mastery before dynamics become a part of the creative process. The moment that students have achieved a modest level of technical mastery with the notes and rhythms the door is open for exploring dynamics and other expressive qualities of the music. Thus, as the technique is refined, there will be a naturalness in the dynamics as opposed to them being "added on" at the last minute or as an afterthought.

Speaking of the creative process, be mindful of the reality that creativity is being viewed more and more as an essential skill, and it must be an integral part of the educational process. Educational authority, lecturer, and author Sir Ken Robinson makes the case that creativity is a critical twenty-

> Be ever mindful of the reality that while essential, playing the correct notes and rhythms is not a manifestation of creativity. Nor is it a demonstration of artistry. (My sermon for the day.)

first-century skill needed to solve today's and the future's pressing problems. Thus, exploring dynamics not only enhances the music making process but also engages students in the creative process that goes beyond the notes and rhythms on the page and is arguably an essential contemporary life skill.

This discussion could also be expanded to consider harmonic content. Perhaps the presence of a deceptive cadence, a suspension, an abrupt dissonance, or other device of surprise that creates harmonic tension could influence our artistic judgment regarding the application of dynamic contrast to highlight the moment.

Subjective considerations abound here as well. Is the music tender? Is there an element of surprise? Perhaps it is a lullaby, a love song, a proclamation of tragedy, or intended to be shocking. Is the music literal, reflective, subtle, or abrasive in content? Each new nuance and musical, perhaps emotional, factor opens the door for more options. I will state the obvious once again: Without reflection, the musical content remains only ink on paper. In this context there remains but one sin; that is, the sin of doing nothing and allowing each note, as Ruth Waterman says, to "play itself."

Now let's explore more options. What other elements of dynamic nuance come into play? Shouldn't the dynamics sustain and reinforce the larger musical gesture? If the answer is yes, then what factors do we have? Maybe there is too much volume too soon, or perhaps the softs are not soft enough to create contrast. Perhaps the dynamic arrival point does not coincide with the melodic or harmonic arrival point. Are the dynamics sustained to the perceived musical destination? There is no end to the variables before us. Thus, subjectivity of dynamic markings and the pacing of dynamics will forever be a formidable challenge. One must approach these artistic decisions as critically and thoughtfully as one would consider the correct fingering of a B-flat on the clarinet or the tuning tendencies of a particular note on a brass instrument.

Let's consult two pieces of music by Frank Ticheli for further enlightenment. First, look at *Amazing Grace*. Examine the dynamic challenges that confront us from measures 83–99. This magnificent final statement of the theme brings every force of the ensemble into play. Because of the crescendo and slight ritardando into measure 83, the band can easily be seduced into pushing the envelope beyond a *forte* dynamic, which while appearing immediately satisfying leaves insufficient dynamic resources to continue the crescendo to the ultimate arrival point in measure 91. In pragmatic terms one must plan ahead and pace the dynamics for maximum expressiveness. If you fail to do so, about all you can do in measure 91 is let your eyes get bigger.

Now look at measure 91 where the next challenge arises. Is the downbeat the arrival point? Is that our musical destination? In truth, one often hears it performed that way followed by a gradual decay of dynamics in the measures that immediately follow. To a degree, that can be musically satisfying, but it appears to me that Ticheli has more to say. Why? In the very next measure the low brass and low woodwinds have quarter note triplets with a crescendo that extends the scope of this climactic moment. There is line and momentum here. Further analysis reveals that the horns have a soaring statement marked expressive in the following measure. To me, the fireworks just keep coming and there is no indication of any diminishment of volume until the decrescendo that begins in measure 96. This is a monolithic moment of musical architecture that last for an entire five measures. Anything less is not as satisfying and is inconsistent with the blueprint Ticheli has given us.

Amazing Grace, mm. 83–98, reduced score in C

Another prime example is found in the last thirteen measures of Frank Ticheli's *Shenandoah*. The dynamic range fluctuates from *forte* to *piano* with a diminuendo to *niente* on the final E-flat major chord. The musical effect can be stunning, perhaps even reverent. But what often happens? Inevitably, the first *mezzo piano* in measure 66 is played too soft. It sounds good and gives the

72

illusion of being musically effective, but from that point forward the music tends to unfold from measure to measure with little or no apparent dynamic contour. Because the first *mezzo piano* is too soft, there is nowhere to go. Thus, by the time the musicians arrive at the final measure, they are already playing so soft that there is literally no way to create the diminuendo into silence that the score calls for.

So, what to do? Consider rehearsing these kinds of dynamic challenges in reverse. Instead of arriving at a randomly chosen dynamic to represent the first *mezzo piano* and then plodding forward hoping for the best, consider first rehearsing the final two measures. Establish a musically appropriate soft dynamic that allows for the clarinets to fade into silence. The ending is now predetermined. With that musical moment in place you have established a reference point by which all other dynamics are defined. You are now ready to go back to measure 66 with a clear aural image of how the dynamics can unfold in order to highlight the multiplicity of subtle arrival points, create discernable dynamic contrasts, and allow for a concluding sense of finality.

Shenandoah, m. 66 to the end, reduced score in C

Certainly, there are other ways to create more compelling dynamic contrasts. Personally, I never hesitate to adjust the number of players at times to widen the dynamic range. The final three measures of the Beeler transcription of Bernstein's *Overture to Candide* offers us a perfect example. Sandwiched between a woodwind plus euphonium *fortissimo* B-flat unison and the final *tutti fortissimo* E-flat major chord is a B-flat dominant seven chord marked *pianissimo*. For the longest time I struggled to get that measure soft enough and light enough to please me; that is, until I asked the ensemble to play that single note one to a part. The contrast was compelling, the lightness was musically appropriate, the ingredients of the B-flat dominant seven chord were clearly heard, and the result beautifully set up the power, impact, and finality of the final E-flat major "shout." It was exactly what I wanted to hear. I now often resort to this strategy in many musical settings when seeking more dramatic dynamic contrast.

In some cases, a fringe benefit of adjusting the number of players to define dynamics also affords one the opportunity to create more clarity and transparency in the harmonic content. A case in point occurs in measures 59–65 in the band version of *Rest* by Frank Ticheli. The vocal text "I shall find the crystal of peace—" is repeated three times in succession. It is stated first *pianissimo*, then *piano* with a slight crescendo and a subtle expansion of instrumentation, and a third time beginning *mezzo forte* with ever expanding forces arriving at a *forte* volume in measure 64.

In order to capture the delicate beauty of this magical moment, I have opted to play the first statement with one player to a part and perform it as soft as possible. Then for the second statement I add an additional player per part and judiciously observe the subtle crescendo. Only on the third and final statement do I default to the full ensemble and build to the measure 64 arrival point. Not only is it an adventitious way to pace the dynamics, but the gradual addition of players enriches the sonority as the ensemble arrives at the final *forte*. The sounds not only become louder, but also more opulent as the music grows. I liken it to the visual experience of watching the twilight sky at dusk and becoming more enthralled as more and more stars begin to fill the heavens.

There is yet another intangible to contemplate in our quest for compelling dynamics: the role of intensity. It is more or less a given that as long as tone quality remains focused, centered, and the issues of balance and blend are properly tended to, intensity is rarely an issue at high volumes. It is simply a natural by-product of the sonic wash of sound being generated.

However, as dynamics soften, tone quality can become fuzzy and unfocused. As it does, there is a natural tendency for intensity to dissipate. One might find a corollary between this phenomenon and the variables we encounter when verbally whispering. Certainly, it is possible to whisper very softly as if sharing a secret with a friend. The words are almost gone by the time they leave our lips. On the other hand, we can also whisper softly with enough intensity to project our words (albeit in a breathy quality) across the room. There is a direct correlation between this sensation of whispering with intensity and what we must capture when playing *pianissimo*.

> Playing soft is not a passive act.

This is not a discussion of pedagogy, but our breath support must be intensified to project the beauty of the moment in a soft but energy-filled and compelling fashion. The bottom line: Playing soft must be infused with a sense of urgency for the compelling emotion present in the music. As conductors and/or performers, we must vigilantly monitor and address this reality.

There is a final factor here that, while obvious to most, is worth noting, that being how distance impacts volume and intensity of sound. Simply put, sound decreases six decibels every time the distance is doubled. For example, dispersing a single source over an area four times larger will be reduced to only a quarter of its original intensity. This is a hard-and-fast law of physics. The bottom line is that the volume of sound you hear on the podium will be very different from what is perceived by the audience. In other words, while what your ears hear is sensed to be beautiful, compelling, vivid colors of sonic contrast, what reaches the ears of the audience might be better described as subtle shades of gray. This phenomenon calls to mind the term "artful exaggeration" referenced earlier. We must be vigilant in creating the most dramatic dynamic contrast possible in order to communicate those contrasts to our listeners.

Let me share a term with you that I feel encapsulates all of the above, that being "dynamic inflection." It was coined by James Boyk, pianist in residence at the California Institute of Technology. It refers to "the natural rise and fall of volume in any communicative sound,"[9] both verbal and musical. He observed that a musical phrase may be marked *forte*, or *piano* for that matter, in the score, but that does not mean that all notes of the phrase are rendered equally. He suggested that there should be an expressive moment-to-moment flexibility in the dynamics. Perhaps this is simply another way to frame Robert Shaw's words that serve as a preamble to this chapter: "The dynamics never sit. They are always in motion." Wonderful words to live by!

Chapter 3

SIN #3: PERCEIVING ALL RHYTHMS LITERALLY

The measurability of musical rhythm, and therefore the accurateness of its notation, is only approximate.
— Bruno Walter[10]

Let's begin with the notion that rhythm is the one indispensable element that is present in all music. It is the singular component of music that organizes all other aspects of our art into a sequential journey through time and over silence. Furthermore, it is the only element of music that can and often does stand alone. Think primal drumming, many forms of chant, and even rap. A more specific example of stand-alone rhythm might be the delightful *Variations on a Handmade Theme* for eight hand clappers by Warren Benson. It is wonderful music but has no musical elements other than rhythm, a few dynamic variables, and some subtle variations in the timbre of the claps. (Check it out if you don't know it!) All of the above are compelling illustrations of music making with no need for melody, harmony, or other elements of music making.

While rhythm can and does exist without melody, there is the antithesis and stark reality that melody cannot subsist without rhythm. The moment melody is created, and possibly laced with harmonic content, there is the immediate necessity for rhythm to provide sequence, structure, and form. But that reality does not dictate that rhythm is the overriding music element thus requiring rigid exactness at every juncture. In truth, there are many circumstances where the melody, harmony, or other musical factors can and do suggest options for how the rhythmic notation might be perceived and interpreted.

Certainly, rhythmic notation appears to be fixed, exact, and finite. A quarter note is a quarter note, an eighth note is an eighth note, and so on. We then match the rhythmic notations to a metronome marking and it would appear that the pathway to refinement is clear. From that vantage point we can easily obsess over rhythmic precision and adopt a mindset of micromanaging every rhythmic detail we see on the page in lockstep. The context of the music matters not.

If for no other reason, that is my rationale for submitting the notion that it is a sin to perceive *all* rhythms literally. Without doubt there is an empirical necessity for some (many) rhythms to be executed with explicit preciseness. I can't imagine Bernstein's "Profanation" from Symphony No. 1, the *Toccata Marziale* of Vaughan Williams, or *Short Ride in a Fast Machine* by John Adams played without a heightened sensitivity to rhythmic accuracy and precision. A compilation of examples in this genre would be endless. But to approach every rhythm in every circumstance and every musical setting with that narrow mindset of unswerving exactness is indeed a musical wrongdoing.

A compelling analogy might be found in the often-heard expression, "Can't see the forest for the trees." The message is the implied reality that if one focuses on the individual trees, he or she will never see or appreciate the beauty of the forest and all that nature has to offer. The observation is generally directed at someone who is too involved in the details of the challenge before them to look at the situation as a whole. In a similar fashion, if you obsess over the exactness of each beat and the absolute preciseness of every rhythm, you run the risk of missing the expansiveness of musical beauty that the relationship and interaction between the notes and the rhythms represents.

So, how do we come to grips with this enigma? When does the musical connotation of the notes override the mathematical exactness that the printed notes suggest? When is rhythmic exactness a deterrent to the musical architecture that is unfolding? In simple terms, when do we get to "color outside the lines" and *interpret* rhythm?

While there could be other and subtler variations of the following, for our discussion let's focus on six specific scenarios:

1. Distorting a written rhythm to highlight a particular musical style.
2. Short notes in dotted rhythms.
3. A single note or note grouping that might be elongated to add nuance to a phrase or an arrival point.
4. An entrance that might be slightly delayed, adding drama, a sense of anticipation, and/or impact.
5. Deliberately stretching the pulse of the music before, during, or after a moment of harmonic emphasis, tension, or resolution.
6. A delayed or blurred release that exceeds the rhythmic exactness of the notation.

DISTORTING A WRITTEN RHYTHM TO HIGHLIGHT A PARTICULAR MUSICAL STYLE

Perhaps the most obvious of all deviations from written rhythmic notation in the contemporary musical world might be the practice of swinging eighth note jazz rhythms. Certainly not a classical music practice, but it is routinely present in the American jazz heritage. The music appears on the page in traditional 3/4 or 4/4 notation, but in actuality the notes and rhythms are performed in a relaxed, swing style quarter note/eighth note configuration that sounds more like 9/8 or 12/8 notation. In some cases, the composer will inscribe instructions to "swing," or the phrase "swing style" will appear in the score or on the parts. But not always. On occasion there is no written indication to swing, but the music begs for that interpretation. You have to go for it!

Similarly, the presence of a flatted third or other "blues notes" in a jazz melody might suggest a subtle rhythmic nuance of that tone. Just enough reflection to highlight its importance. If one just plods through that beat in lockstep with an unwavering pulse or rigid allegiance to the throb of a metronome, the magic of the moment is lost. Look no further than the music of George Gershwin to see countless examples of this musical idiosyncrasy.

Are there moments for the application of this subtlety outside the world of jazz? Certainly. For example, there are moments of expressive drama in many Spanish marches (*Paso Dobles*) that beg to be elongated to fully capture stylistic characteristics of this elegant march style. Or in any music where one might "hang on" to the peak note of a musical phrase to embrace its beauty or elegance. In simplest terms, these moments implore you to play the music rather than simply regurgitate the notes in a rigid, expressionless fashion.

SHORT NOTES IN DOTTED RHYTHMS

To expand on the quote from Bruno Walter that opens this chapter, the maestro went on to say: "Divergence from arithmetical exactness occurs mainly in the case of the short notes in dotted rhythms, which an interpreter of lively rhythmic sense feels a little shorter, and therefore places a little later than prescribed by notation."[11] (Note that he uses the word "mainly" as opposed to "only," thus suggesting that there can be other deviations as well.)

There are many examples where a slight departure from rhythmic exactness might be appropriate. Look no further than "Lisbon," the first movement of *Lincolnshire Posy* by Percy Grainger. As we all know, the time signature is a straightforward 6/8 marked dotted quarter note = ca. 116, accompanied by the suggestion that the music be performed briskly with plenty of lilt. In fine print at the bottom of the Frederick Fennell edition is the clarification that lilt be interpreted as meaning beats one and four should be played much heavier than beats three and six.

Adherence to these parameters will certainly result in a more authentic interpretation of this movement, but I propose there is additional rationale to consider. Look at the first line of the text.

'Tis on the Monday morning all in the month of May.

Now let's underscore the words that would correspond with the eighth notes in Grainger's score.

'Tis on the Monday morning all in the month of May.

If one reads those words aloud in a natural, spontaneous 6/8 fashion, there tends to be a jerky quality to the rhythm, and the underscored words tend to be pronounced later than where they would fall in a perfectly subdivided 6/8 rhythm. In fact, in an earlier piano sketch of this music the composer interjected the word "jumpingly" to describe the style when the second half of the tune comes in.

More evidence that supports this interpretation can be found in the wax cylinder recordings accompanying Robert Garofalo's *Folk Songs and Dances in Lincolnshire Posy*. The compact disc contains two recorded versions of "Lisbon," and in the recording of folk singers John Roberts and Tony Barrand in particular, the eighth notes are slightly delayed in a fashion that might be best described as a unique rhythm living somewhere between a quarter note–eighth note pattern in 6/8 and a dotted eighth note–sixteenth note rhythm in 2/4. Call it what you will, it seems to capture the earthy, spontaneous rhythmic quirkiness of a folk singer's natural, unique style, thus making it totally appropriate for a compelling interpretation of this one-minute-and-twenty-second masterpiece. Is it rhythmically precise? No. Does it adhere to the rules of rhythm? No. Is it music? Absolutely!

To put it another way, I'm confident that an accomplished folk song singer rendering these kinds of heartfelt tunes is not thinking in the back of their mind, "subdivide, subdivide, subdivide." No! They are allowing the text and the spontaneity of the moment guide the rhythmic DNA of the music.

For those who may not be familiar, *Folk Songs and Dances in Lincolnshire Posy* by conductor and scholar Robert Garofalo is an incomparable collection of resources all directly related to Grainger's masterpiece. Included are complete vocal versions (music and text) of all the sourced folk music, historical and interpretive notes, and a compact disc featuring multiple renditions of all songs and dances as well as recordings of Grainger speaking, singing, and playing. It is published by Whirlwind Music Publications.

Another example familiar to all of us is the march from *Symphonic Metamorphosis of Themes by Carl Maria von Weber* by Paul Hindemith, transcribed for band by Keith Wilson. A predominant rhythm throughout is the traditional dotted eighth note–sixteenth note pattern. If approached literally, one would dutifully place the sixteenth note precisely on the fourth sixteenth note of each quarter note pulse. The notes would receive equal emphasis and every note would dutifully align with the click of the metronomic subdivision. Certainly, this would be rhythmically exact, and you can readily hear performances of the march that are indeed correct but, to my ear, fail to capture the vigor and vibrancy of this amazing music.

To me there is a musical urgency present that supersedes the notation on the printed page. Perhaps the relationship between the sixteenth note and the note that follows (often another dotted eighth note) and the inevitability of the overall musical line is more important than the exact rhythmic placement of the sixteenth note. Thus, if the sixteenth note is placed closer to the following dotted eighth note and enhanced with a slight emphasis, its relationship with the following note and the overall momentum of the music is greatly enhanced. A driving force is created that seems to be totally in concert with Hindemith's musical intent and consistent with the words of Bruno Walter cited at the beginning of the chapter.

There is a second rationale for this approach that adds validity for me personally. It is the presence of the occasional triplet rhythm that is interspersed throughout many of the phrases. If the triplet is played rhythmically precise (and it should be) and the sixteenth note is ever so slightly late and played with emphasis as proposed above, the contrast between the rhythms becomes more vivid and, in my way of thinking, more captivating.

A perusal of recordings of this work will reveal many variations as to the treatment of the dotted rhythms. In virtually every case there is a consistency with the rhythm within the context of that specific recording, but a clear, subtle difference can be heard from recording to recording. Many are uniquely compelling; however, those that adhere precisely to the rhythmic accuracy of a mechanical dotted eighth–sixteenth tend to possess a stilted quality. As in so much music making, the beauty is that there can be more than one right answer, and the underlying factor always present is the overall musical intent as opposed to the exact execution of a singular musical element; in this case, rhythmic preciseness. Remember the overriding importance of looking at the entire forest and not just the individual trees.

As further evidence of this phenomenon, one needs only to listen to an orchestral performance of this movement of *Symphonic Metamorphosis of Themes by Carl Maria von Weber* with Hindemith conducting. His interpretation clearly validates the appropriateness of capturing the essence of the music as opposed to being content with a rhythmic replication of the printed page.

This approach to dotted rhythms is not a recent phenomenon. There is evidence of this performance practice throughout music history. Leopold Mozart in 1756 wrote that dotted rhythms are poorly served by notation. To paraphrase, he said that the dotted note should be held rather longer, and the shorter notes played more rapidly so the performance does not sound too "sleepy." That about sums it up!

A Single Note or Note Grouping that Might Be Elongated to Add Nuance to a Phrase or an Arrival Point

Our music is full of those magic moments where a slight hesitation or distortion of the actual rhythm creates a moment of stunning beauty. As an example, take a look at measures 162–163 of *Ballad for Band* by Morton Gould. There is nothing but whole notes and half notes, which is easily played perfectly in rhythm if one has mastered the first few pages of a beginning band method book.

The arrival point is a warm, luxurious E-flat major chord that is preceded by a lush, rich predominantly woodwind G-flat-9 chord. This is arguably the most magical moment in the entire piece. Other than the word "slower" leading into measure 161, there is no objective reference to any tempo variation until measure 164. If one plays the ink, the notes will be performed with measured consistency and an expectation for rhythmic accuracy will be met. I have heard it performed that way on countless occasions.

But is there a sin here? I would propose that the music can be elevated to a whole new level of artistry if time metaphorically stands still in measure 163, thus creating a sense of anticipation and resolution when the E-flat major chord is finally sounded. Delaying the moment that the E-flat tonality washes over the players and listeners might be compared to that sensation that occurs when one exhales with a sigh, thus creating a sense of resolution that is lost if the notes unfold literally and with rhythmic exactness.

Let's look at another example embedded in a totally different contextual setting. In the middle, slow section of *Blue Shades* by Frank Ticheli, with a tempo marking of 60 BPM, there is a pivotal moment at measure 304. The slow blues section has been unfolding for roughly a minute when the focus morphs from transparent predominantly woodwind colorations to a full-blown quasi-jazz ensemble. The composer's only indication of musical intent is the presence of the word "dirty" at the top of the score.

Let's pause for a moment and think about the meaning of the adjective "dirty." What might the composer have in mind? The dictionary tells us it means "covered or marked with an unclean substance." Synonyms include such words as "soiled," "grimy," "grubby," and even "vulgar."

So, with that definition in mind, should there be more than just getting the notes and rhythms right? Do we want this transition to retain the preceding style, or does something need to happen here to elevate the drama? Certainly, the option exists to plod on in a 12/8 blues style observing the already established 60 clicks per minute. No harm, no foul. But what if we opt to once again "color outside the lines" where the art lives? I'm thinking "down and dirty." What if we, to a degree, forgo rhythmic exactness and precise tempo? What if we begin to broaden the tempo a little in the measure or two in front of measure 304? And above all, what if we delay the downbeat of measure 304 as long as possible, making the listener wait just a moment longer to hear the music swagger across the bar line as if the gates of hell just opened? The resolution then becomes more satisfying and then we proceed at a slightly slinkier tempo. Herein lies the potential to capture the essence of this pivotal moment. Let's face it, people. This is stripper music!

In his own words, Ticheli states, "I would say it doesn't just add nuance. It heightens expectations by making the listener wait just a moment longer. It heightens tension, and then when the goal is finally reached, the resolution is made even more satisfying because of that extra moment of waiting created." Take Ticheli's words to heart. They are gospel! One can apply them to countless musical scenarios far beyond those referenced in this discussion.

An Entrance that Might Be Slightly Delayed, Adding Drama, a Sense of Anticipation, and/or Impact

There are countless examples of this inevitability throughout all music. Just as one might delay the utterance of a pivotal word when speaking, a slight hesitation in the placement of a note fosters anticipation and perhaps interjects a sense of drama.

Let's consider the first stanza of Charles Anthony Silvestri's stunning poem "Sleep," so beautifully set for voices by Eric Whitacre (and then later scored for winds by the composer).

> The evening hangs beneath the moon,
> A silver thread on darkened dune.
> With closing eyes and resting head
> I know that sleep is coming soon.

The composer eloquently sets these powerfully enthralling words to a straightforward array of quarter notes, half notes, dotted half notes, and a final whole note that, to me, adds shape and reflection to the text. In the band transcription, students could master this phrase rhythmically in their first year of music instruction. Simply turn on the metronome, pat one's foot, and in all likelihood rhythmic accuracy will soon follow. But what about the meaning of the text and the use of lush dissonances that begs reflection? Holistically the music begins to take on a new, deeper level of expressiveness. While still of importance, the exactness of the rhythm becomes subordinate to the ebb and flow of text and the overpowering expressiveness of the music. By necessity, musical reflection as opposed to rhythmic perfection becomes central to the artistic realization of the score.

This rhythmic fluctuation is not found only in slow music. Even marches offer opportunity for rhythmic inexactness. A prime example is John Philip Sousa's march *Semper Fidelis*, which, by the way, Sousa considered to be his finest march. In the first measure, third measure, and measure 9 there is a *tutti* quarter note on beat two. Certainly, it is rhythmically correct to place that note precisely on beat two of the measure. The result is rhythmically concise, clear, and energetic. And it is certainly correct. But what if that beat is ever so slightly delayed or perhaps the note is thought of as being placed on the back side of the beat? With the presence of that slight hesitation the drama of these arrival notes is subtly exaggerated and certainly more impactful. A sense of swagger or cockiness is created that would be very appropriate for a march honoring the men and women of the United States Marine Corps. Is it right? Is it wrong? I will leave that decision to others, but certainly it is an interpretation that factors more than just a rhythmic beat into the precise execution of these powerful notes.

Similarly, the style of the march *British Eighth* by Zo Elliott tempts the conductor to move from beat to beat with a slightly delayed pulse. This march begs to be played "on the heels" or the back side of each beat from the first downbeat to the final note. The result is music that gives the illusion of being stately and perhaps even a little pompous. And it simply feels right. The bottom line? Elements other than precise rhythms are influencing the final interpretation of the music.

DELIBERATELY STRETCHING THE PULSE OF THE MUSIC BEFORE, DURING, OR AFTER A MOMENT OF HARMONIC EMPHASIS, TENSION, OR RESOLUTION

While this application of rhythmic inexactness seems so evident and fundamental, the reality exists that all too often our obsession with keeping time and achieving rhythmic exactness gets in the way of this kind of musical beauty.

Let's start with a very straightforward example. Prior to the United States of America's bicentennial, the United States Marine Band commissioned Clare Grundman to write a piece to commemorate that momentous occasion. Grundman's response was *Concord*, featuring three traditional tunes found in the music of early New England. For the record, it was premiered at the 1987 Conference of the World Association of Symphonic Bands and Ensembles in Boston.

The center section of *Concord* is based on "America" by William Billings. No, this is not the familiar "America" that we know and love today. This tuneful hymn was written by Billings to reflect the independent spirit of a new nation. The melody is simple, tuneful, and beautifully conceived. The primary harmonic focal point of Grundman's treatment of this hymn is the reoccurrence of lushly scored G major and C major four-three suspensions woven into the harmonic fabric of the music. Once again, it is certainly correct to play those rhythms precisely and in rigid lockstep tempo. I personally have heard it played "by the book" in that fashion often.

But in doing so, what is missing? Does that exactness allow for the drama of the harmonic content to unfold? Absolutely not! In some form or fashion there must be reflection on the drama that is created by the tension and resolution of the fourth above the bass note coming to rest on the third of the chord. Call it nuance, expressiveness, artistic license, or what you may, but these musical moments beg for some subtle rhythmic distortion. Notes must be stretched or the rhythmic exactness must be blurred in order to highlight these musical moments. How much? You must answer that question. There are no rules. In reality you have three beats to consider: the third beat of the previous measure that sets up the suspension, beat one of the following measure that triggers the suspension, and the next beat that heralds the resolution. The rhythmic accuracy of all three beats is eligible for a less rhythmic interpretation that could lead to increased drama and a more musically satisfying outcome. The degree of rhythmic distortion is up to you and subject only to your musical judgment. The ultimate sin here is to focus singularly on the rhythmic exactness without paying homage to the lushness of the harmony that is unfolding.

At the risk of oversimplification, it boils down to the following:

- Lengthening beat three entices the listener to anticipate what is about to come.
- Stretching beat one of the next measure intensifies the tension of the suspension (another example of the role of anticipation referenced earlier).
- An elongation of beat two allows the listener to bathe in the warmth of the resolution.

Certainly, there could be some combination of these three options further enhanced by a slight infusion of dynamic contrast. Doing so dramatically enriches the expressiveness of the notes on the page. Embrace these moments with your heart and your musical soul, not your head. To do any less is an artistic failing.

Another example of where this approach would be very musically appropriate is in the case of a deceptive cadence being sounded in lieu of an authentic cadence; that is, a dominant chord moving to a VI chord as opposed to the expected resolution to the tonic or root chord. A prime example is the G minor chord in measure 152 of *An American Elegy* by Frank Ticheli. The progression is totally unexpected and serves to add an elevated level of drama to the music. Yes, in this case the composer has indicated a ritardando leading into the deceptive resolution, but musically speaking, even if there were no composer guidance on the printed page, the musical result would be the same. There would be a broadening of tempo to elevate anticipation for the musical surprise that is about to occur.

A Delayed or Blurred Release that Exceeds the Rhythmic Exactness of the Notation

In a musical world that is preoccupied with rhythmic accuracy and precision, it is easy to be seduced into a mindset that focuses only on the neatness and/or exactness of each release. Of course, in many cases that is a commendable goal. After all, who wants to hear sloppy or ragged releases? But there are many occasions where this strategy is detrimental to the overarching musical intent of the moment. In such cases, rhythmic exactness and steady pulse are subordinate to more compelling, but sometimes subtle and less evident, musical considerations. Let's examine some examples.

Particularly in lyrical music, notes that evaporate into silence need not end abruptly or be rhythmically precise. Let's examine a brilliant illustration of this phenomenon. The music is *Rippling Watercolors* by Brian Balmages. In the words of the composer, "This was not meant to be a lyrical piece for younger ensembles; rather, it was written as a fully expressive lyrical work that *happens* to be played by younger ensembles." (Author's note: We need more music like this!) As you peruse the score you will see an abundance of reflective phrases that culminate in moments of absolute silence. These phrase endings resolving into rests should not culminate in precise releases, but rather the ending notes should simply fade into the silence. (Often, I simply tell students to "smear" the note into the silence.) The note just disappears.

Furthermore, the compelling silences that follow should not be viewed as a concise number of precisely metered beats of silence, but rather there should be a rhythmically void interlude of silence that timelessly floats to the next entrance. Such moments can be viewed as an interim of reflective silence. If this music unfolds to the tick of a metronome or an obsession with rhythmic pulse, the magic of the music is lost. Certainly, the notes are played but no music is made. A musical transgression for sure.

This subjective consideration is equally applicable in one's approach to the interpretation of instrumental transcriptions of choral music. A paramount example can be found in the H. Robert Reynolds's transcription of *O Magnum Mysterium* by Morten Lauridsen. A perusal of the vocal score, in Latin of course, reveals that with rare exception each phrase ending of the text comes to rest on a vowel or a soft, round syllable such as *-um*, *-le*, *-pio*, and *-la*. What does this tell us? Is there something here that should guide our nuance of these releases? This actuality suggests to me that the precise release of these notes is subordinate to the imperative that each of these phrase endings be rounded, gentle, and, in some instances, subdued, perhaps "smearing" the release into the silence that follows, as previously referenced. The focus shifts from an obsession with *when* the notes end to an artful treatment of *how* the notes will end and melt into nothing. In more poetic terms, the music might be viewed as flowing pastels as opposed to neatly organized primary colors. With this kind of lyrical music, perhaps the text is a far better reference for how these rhythms unfold as opposed to the exactness of the notes one sees on the page. A failure to do so is a wrongdoing.

In Summary

Are there specific hard-and-fast rules that apply to any of the above? Absolutely not. As is often said, one of the beauties of music making is that we have the option to live in an artistic world that affords us bountiful opportunities to be guided not only by our hands and our heads, but also by our heart and our musical soul. Thus, what we have discussed here might be best described as options for artistry. The depth of our musicianship is partially determined by how we ponder these rhythmic subtleties and the judgments we make to factor them into our music making. In truth, the ultimate sin is to focus only on the objectivity of the rhythms and to make no interpretive judgment at all.

CHAPTER 4

SIN #4: BEING OBSESSED WITH TEMPO MARKINGS

A good tempo is a discovery.
— Bruce Adolphe[12]

There is likely no fundamental element of music making that is debated more profusely or passionately than tempo. Regardless of the musical genre—be it classical, pop, jazz, or electronic—tempo remains a paramount consideration. This reality is universally true whether we are talking about composers, performers, or conductors. Many would argue that tempo selection is crucial, as the speed of the music can dictate or at least influence many, if not all, other elements of music. Certainly, articulation, phrasing, musical style, and even where we might breathe can be affected by tempo selection.

Thus, finding the *right* tempo remains a high priority in any music making enterprise. But if indeed there is a "right" tempo, does that suggest that all other tempos would be wrong? I think not! In truth, even composers, as we shall see, sometimes take their own music faster or slower than the speeds they imagined when assigning a tempo on the score, or over time they change their mind about the "right" tempo.

In truth, different people inevitably perform music at different speeds, and sometimes the same person at different speeds from day to day. Thus, there can be a variety of "right" tempos all hinging on a multitude of factors and variables, including but not limited to an objective assessment of the tempo markings, tempered by thoughtful consideration of the composers intent, and perhaps most important, a personal, informed, intuitive musical judgment on the part of the conductor or performer. Perhaps tempo is like water; it seeks and discovers its own level. As composer, author, lecturer, and performer Bruce Adolphe so eloquently states, "A good tempo is a discovery."

So, where is the sin in all of this? How can you commit a transgression when there are no hard-and-fast boundaries to observe or clearly defined rules to follow? Perhaps a sin is committed when we embrace an external observance of tempo markings that pays allegiance only to the mechanical, objective, measurable speed of the music. With that approach, if the tempo marking dictates 120 beats per minute, then that is what the tempo must be. No further assessment is required. Turn the metronome on and get to work!

Regardless of the factors and forces that come into play, the objective should be to discover an internal, heartfelt connection with the music that makes the pace of the music feel natural, alive, and expressive. To put it another way, the question before us is: How does one connect with a tempo range that fits the style, mood, and message of the music?

As we proceed, let's be clear that we are talking specifically about the tempo at which the music could be performed or is being performed. Possible correlations with the topics of rhythm and meter will remain outside the parameters of our discussion.

There is more about these topics elsewhere.

So, what is the big deal? After all, one can argue that tempo can be addressed very objectively. Over centuries, tempo indications such as Adagio, Andante, and Allegro have evolved. However, let's be reminded that these are all Italian terms, and when literally translated they have very little to do with speed but rather a sense of musical style and feeling. Consider these few examples:

- Largo: copious, abundant, full
- Adagio: at ease
- Moderato: moderate
- Allegro: lively, gay, cheerful
- Vivace: brisk, vigorous

The number of words that frame these terms could easily be endless. And the more words inserted into the discussion, the more blurred the parameters can become.

These traditional, universally recognized descriptors are often given more specificity by applying adjectives such as *molto, meno, poco,* or *non troppo.* But in truth there remains no exactness in any of these terms. At best they simply suggest an approximation of the "right" tempo, and we must take these somewhat vague directives and arrive at a tempo that allows us to bring the music to life in our own personal way while remaining faithful to the composer's intent.

While there had been previous attempts to create a timekeeping device, it was in 1815 that Johann Maelzel patented what he described as "a machine for the improvement of all musical performance." For the first time we had a functional instrument that measured time in beats per minute. Surely such a device would be expected to eliminate the vagueness and ambiguity while

Beethoven was among the first composers to utilize metronome markings in a composition. But even to this day there is debate as to the accuracy of Beethoven's metronome and, in turn, the musical validity of the tempo markings he indicated.

giving us a definitive reference for tempo. After all, how could someone argue with an objective measurement of beats per minute?

But variables in tempo remain to this day. Let's consider the tempo marking "Allegro." Depending on where you look, you will discover the following suggested parameters.

- One reference source: MM = 84–144
- Another reference source: MM = 120–168
- A nineteenth-century Maelzel metronome: MM = 120
- A 1950 electric metronome suggests: MM = 116
- The app on my iPhone indicates: MM = 110–132

There is a variance from a precise 120 indication to a range differentiation of 60 beats per minute—all under the umbrella of Allegro. Similar discrepancies exist for all tempo markings. There is simply no definitive guide that empirically translates a tempo marking into beats per minute. Subjectivity, artistic expression, and some pragmatic factors simply prohibit that reality.

Let's pause here to note that in many contemporary settings the traditional term "metronome marking," indicated as "MM," is being replaced with the more authentic term "beats per minute," or "BPM." This is especially true in electronic music and in the recording studio, where a tempo marking as specific as 124.5 BPM is not uncommon. And we have the technology to relentlessly monitor that musical pace. Personally, I'm not convinced this is a good thing. But for our purposes the traditional MM indication and the more contemporary BPM will be used interchangeably.

While considering all of the above, the fact remains that the variables in considering tempo are, to a great extent, limitless. To begin with, there can be discrepancies from the composer's point of view, even in simple, supposedly straightforward music. As a case in point, consider the first movement of the young band classic *Three Ayres from Gloucester* by Hugh M. Stuart. The time signature is cut time with a tempo marking of Allegretto (MM = 96). Yet most references would suggest what we have is a contradiction in terms in that MM = 96 would be slightly on the slow side for a traditional Allegretto marking. So, is it Allegretto or is it MM = 96? That is the genesis of this discussion and is, of course, for you to decide. For me personally, this music plays well up around MM = 108. A few clicks above MM = 96 seems to bring the music to life, and that increased tempo is very much in the "sweet spot" for an Allegretto tempo marking.

This is one of many examples where multiple variables and/ or the subtle nuance of individuals can and do come into play, the result being a compelling argument for the necessity of contemplating the artistry of what we do as opposed to the craft of what we do.

I vividly remember attending a wind ensemble music conference at Yale in 1976. This was the seventh in a series of groundbreaking wind ensemble music conferences that took place between 1970 and 1977. These meetings were championed by the newly emerging young leadership of the wind band movement that was recalibrating the trajectory of the wind band medium. These emerging artists were often affectionately referred to as "the turtleneck gang" because of their propensity for turtleneck sweaters. (And more than a few smoked pipes.) It is arguable that these annual gatherings served as the genesis of what we know and embrace today as the modern wind band.

One of the speakers at that conference was Keith Wilson, who was on faculty at Yale for over forty years as professor of woodwinds, clarinet in particular, and also severed as director of bands. For many years he worked alongside Paul Hindemith, and at Hindemith's request he transcribed the *Symphonic Metamorphosis on Themes of Carl Maria von Weber* for concert band. Today, that transcription is viewed by many as one of the masterpieces of our repertoire.

As a part of Keith Wilson's lecture, he shared his account of an occasion when Paul Hindemith came to Wilson and informed him that he was composing a new work and was hoping that Wilson would assemble an ensemble to prepare a first reading of the piece. In his lecture, Wilson went into great lengths to articulate the overwhelming sense of challenge and responsibility he felt in fulfilling the request of this iconic composer. He assured the attendees at his lecture that he agonized over every note, every marking, and every nuance of Hindemith's new composition.

Then the big day arrived, and Hindemith came to the venue where the reading was to take place. He positioned himself at the back of the hall and prepared to hear his new creation come to life for the first time. Wilson gave the downbeat and the music began to unfold. In only a matter of measures he heard Hindemith's voice booming from the back of the hall as he hurried down the aisle, repeating over and over, "Stop! Stop! The tempo is all wrong." In the conversation that followed at the edge of the stage, Hindemith insisted that the tempo was too slow and had to move forward. Wilson shared with his lecture attendees that he quickly retorted to the composer, "But, Paul, we are playing at exactly the tempo you indicated in your score." Wilson said that Hindemith immediately countered, "Don't play the tempo that is marked. Play the tempo that is right!"

We have no way of knowing today what the overriding factors might have been that caused Hindemith to respond as he did, but without question, in his mind, the power of the music superseded the tempo markings on the page. Failing to find the right tempo was indeed a sin.

In yet another scenario, I vividly recall Francis McBeth, the renowned band composer, preparing a performance of one of his own works for an honor band concert. Many band directors were present observing the rehearsal. At one point in the music he insisted on a tempo that was dramatically contrary to the tempo marking on the score. Later, when asked about it, he informed us that when he submitted that score to Southern Music Company, his publisher, he had failed to indicate a metronome marking at that point in the music. He went on to tell us that when the publisher contacted him to address the omission, he sang a few measures of the music in his head and suggested a tempo marking. That tempo marking was added to the score, a tempo that, in reality, turned out to be totally incompatible with the composer's musical intent for that moment. To McBeth's chagrin, that tempo marking was taken as gospel by countless band directors and replicated in countless concert and festival performances. Yet when he conducted the work it was clear that his musical, creative judgment superseded the tempo he mistakenly proposed for the score. He insisted on the "right" tempo.

I personally remember a very similar experience while serving as director of bands at Baylor University. As a part of our composer-in-residence series we enjoyed the priceless luxury of having a major composer collaborate with us each year. On one such occasion we had the good fortune of having famed composer Samuel Adler on the Baylor campus. At the time he was in the midst of his twenty-nine-year tenure on the composition faculty at the Eastman School of Music. The piece of his music I was preparing with the Baylor Wind Ensemble was *Southwestern Sketches*. It was commissioned in 1961 to celebrate the fiftieth anniversary of New Mexico's statehood. I had performed it once before and was eager to perform it again in collaboration with the composer. The composition was groundbreaking at the time and was Adler's first work for wind band as well. (Unfortunately, *Southwestern Sketches* has not survived the test of time and is rarely heard today.)

Commensurate with Keith Wilson's expectations for his collaboration with Hindemith, it was my personal desire to be scrupulously true to the printed score in every way. The final section of the twelve-minute work is in cut time with a metronome marking of MM = 120. We prepared accordingly. Then the day came and Adler took the podium for his rehearsal. For the most part he was pleased with our preparation and from my point of view everything was going nicely. Then he arrived at measure 259 and the tempo marking of Allegro, half note = 120. The tempo he took was easily twenty clicks faster than the tempo marking, approaching MM = 144. The poor woodwinds looked like deer in headlights. The room was filled with paralyzed surprise, but after several restarts they began to rise to the challenge he had placed before them.

At some point I felt compelled to make the observation that we had prepared the finale at the tempo he had indicated in the score. He very nicely responded that he realized he was going faster than the tempo he had indicated but that over time he had concluded that the musical content suggested a much faster tempo. (Knowing that in advance would have been helpful.) There was a lot of late-night practice by woodwind players that evening, but by the time of the performance they had successfully mastered his new tempo.

In hindsight, Samuel Adler was right; at the quicker tempo the music took on an aura of excitement and vitality that simply was not present at the original tempo. As in previous examples, he had determined the tempo that was right as opposed to observing the tempo that was marked.

These comparable yet distinctly unique accounts prompt a discussion of what we might refer to as intuitive musical judgment, that being the act of determining a tempo based on what one feels about the music and guided by one's inherent, intrinsic musicality. H. Robert Reynolds shared with me a story of his experience with the great American composer Aaron Copland during his years as director of bands at Long Beach State University. The account, in Reynolds's own words, goes like this:

> At the dress rehearsal, I turned to Copland and said, "I know I am going at a slightly different tempo from the one you marked for this section, and I certainly will go at 'your tempo,' but I really feel it at the slightly slower tempo." Copland then said to me, "If I were conducting it, I would go at the tempo I indicated, but I want you to go at the tempo that feels right to you."

Wow!

In summary, consider the following. There is a singular, defining message revealed in each scenario. Hindemith wanted the "right" tempo. McBeth had "gotten it wrong." Adler had "changed his mind." Copland affirmed the reality that there could be "more than one musically appropriate tempo."

I rest my case.

Let me share with you an overwhelmingly evocative example of how a tempo can change over time. Take a moment from your reading to listen to two contrasting performances of *The Goldberg Variations*, BWV 988, by J. S. Bach. *The Goldberg Variations* remain one of the great masterpieces of all time, and readily available on YouTube are two different performances of this work by Glenn Gould, one of the greatest concert pianists of all times. The differences in the two performances are striking. The first was recorded in June 1955 when Gould was only twenty-two years old. The performance is technically stunning, self-assertive, and perhaps even a bit flamboyant. Wonderful music making by any measure!

Now contrast that exuberant, youthful performance with the recording that Gould did some twenty-six years later in 1981, only a year before his death. The dramatic differences are profound and, in some ways, defy description as the music unfolds at a slower, much more reflective pace. What a difference a quarter of a century made in this musical genius' approach to the exact same notes and rhythms! This is the music making of a deeply reflective older human being, a musician who has been to the mountaintop, an artist who has lived and flourished at the most sacred alters of music making.

Is one tempo right and the other tempo wrong? Absolutely not! They both beautifully define where Gould was on his life journey at two distinctively different points of time. I would argue that both tempos are perfect.

There are countless other perspectives. At a recent music conference, I had the good fortune to hear John Mackey discuss his music and share his thoughts on the matter of tempo markings. Interestingly, he made it very clear that the faster the tempo marking in his music, the more insistent he was that the tempo marking indicated be observed. For example, the tempo for *Undertow* is quarter note = 160 BPM. To him, that is the tempo where that music lives. The tempo at Letter E in *Aurora Awakes* is very specifically quarter note = 124 BPM. Yet in other places Mackey gives a tempo range such as quarter note = 164–178 BPM. But it was clear in his comments that to a great extent in his fast music a specified tempo or tempo window was non-negotiable.

On the other hand, he stated that there could be more liberties with tempo variations in his slower music. He affirms this reality in the opening of *Aurora Awakes*. In contrast to his specific tempo marking at measure 69, he indicates a slow and free tempo of quarter note = circa 68 at the beginning. Thus, he gives permission for a little tempo wiggle room.

There is additional evidence of this tempo freedom in his stunning slow work *This Cruel Moon*. In that setting he suggests a tempo marking of quarter note = 56 BPM, rubato throughout. He then goes on to define the duration of the piece to be six to seven-and-a-half minutes depending on interpretation. That is a ninety-second variation in performance time for a piece of that length, thus opening a broad range of possibilities for interpretation. The term "artistic license" comes to mind.

The underlying message here might be the reality that the more you know about the composer, the more you understand their priorities and intent; and the more intimately you connect with their music, the greater the likelihood that a musical connection between the composer and conductor will emerge.

Personal preferences can come into play as well. *Children's March* by Percy Grainger, for instance, is an example. In the Southern Music Company edition, edited by R. Mark Rogers, the tempo marking reads "Fairly fast. M.M. dotted quarter note = about 126." In a conversation with the editor, Rogers noted that Grainger's tempo marking is consistent in the band, orchestra, duo piano, and solo piano versions of the work. You can certainly hear performances that are at or above that 126 BPM marking. Such interpretations easily capture the playful, joyful spirit of the music. But to my ear a slightly slower tempo allows the many small, subtle moments embedded in almost every measure to be more defined and enjoyed by the listener. The music simply sounds more settled and perhaps even a little cocky. The slightly slower tempo allows more time to savor the intricate and subtle musical interplays. Even Grainger, in a recording of the two pianos–four hands version, embraces a tempo closer to 120 BPM. To me, the natural tempo for *Children's March* is somewhere in the 116–118 BPM range. An analogy might be the act of reading a piece of poetry. Often reading the words less rapidly allows for more reflection on the subtle and sometimes obscure relevance and artistry of the text.

Now, can there be pragmatic considerations that influence tempo selection? In some cases, I absolutely think so. Let's consider a few.

First, in music that is technically complex or music that is full of multiple lines and trending polyphonic in nature, I am sometimes inclined to take a tempo that is a few clicks slower in an effort to achieve more clarity and allow the multiple lines to more fluently intertwine. Also, the music tends to sound less frantic if I can find a slightly relaxed tempo that seems more natural. This is especially true with larger ensembles. Even in marches such as *In Storm and Sunshine* by J. C. Heed I am going to opt for a slower tempo with an eighty-five-piece concert band than I might choose for a sprightlier wind ensemble. And this decision has little or nothing

> The tempo is the suitcase. If the suitcase is too small, everything is completely wrinkled. If the tempo is too fast, everything becomes so scrambled you can't understand it.
>
> — Daniel Barenboim

to do with technique. To my ear it is all about clarity and an awareness of musical intent.

The same strategy might apply when considering the acoustics of a venue. In a performance space with a lot of reverb I will opt to consider a slower tempo with "busy" music in an effort to let the music "swim around" in the resonance of the hall. And, as a sidebar, I'm also inclined to shorten the note length in highly articulated music in this acoustical environment to aid in the clarity.

There is a corollary to this logic in slow music where musical line (another potential sin discussed elsewhere) must be considered. I vividly remember working with an outstanding high school band of younger players that was preparing a transcription of a slow, sustained choral work. The performance tempo the conductor had chosen was deadly slow. While technically accurate, the students had no chance to understand, feel, or create a musical line. They simply plodded from note to note and measure to measure. I encouraged the director to move the tempo forward slightly so there was some flow and direction to the music. It made all the difference in the world. The music started to come to life and the students started to get it.

Later after rehearsal I ask the director what factors led to the selection of the slower tempo. The response was, "That's the tempo the Dallas Winds perform it." I quickly but gently made the observation, "You know, you are a wonderful teacher and you have amazing students, but they are not the artists that comprise the Dallas Winds." Her youthful students simply didn't have the musical maturity or artistic depth to sustain and feel the musicality of the expansive phrases and musical line at that very mature tempo.

At this point perhaps our discourse should return to a discussion of the metronome and its role in the process of selecting and monitoring tempo. While the metronome is an essential tool, it is just that. It is a machine, a machine that measures nothing more and nothing less than beats per minute. And it is absolutely void of any expressiveness. The click, click, click, or beep, beep, beep remains the same regardless of the music it is monitoring. Yet in our highly objectified world there is strong temptation to surrender our musical soul and artistic values to the relentless throb of the metronome.

Perhaps Daniel Gregory Mason said it best. To put his credibility in context, he was the son of Henry Mason, founder of the Mason & Hamlin Piano Company. His grandfather was hymn composer Lowell Mason and co-founder of public school music education in the United States. Daniel Gregory Mason was a composer in his own right, a faculty member at Columbia University, and the author of numerous books and teaching guides. This is what he said:

> To play with the metronome is to play mechanically—the reason being, of course, that we are then playing by the measure, or rather by the beat, instead of by the phrase. . . . Mathematical exactitude gives us a dead body in place of the living musical organism with its ebb and flow of rhythmical energy.[13]

William James, principal percussionist with the St. Louis Symphony, shares a slightly different, more contemporary but equally relevant spin on the topic. He says that while the metronome is one of the most valuable tools a musician can use, he prefers not to use beats per minute to define tempo. He goes on to say that if he has a clear image in his head of the style, attitude, and musical goals, he can actually arrive at his ideal tempo more often than if he tries objectively to pull 115 BPM right out of the air. The focus should be on musical ideas rather than tempo markings.

Do these salient points of view suggest that there is no place for the metronome in our musical world? Absolutely not! By any measure, the metronome is a valuable and, in many cases, essential device. Personally, I rarely study a score without having a metronome close at hand. But, at the same time, I resist the temptation to immediately reference the metronome to establish the composer's requested tempo. I want the music to speak to me as opposed to isolating and objectifying the tempo by mechanical means. I much prefer to allow all of the musical elements to swim around in my head until they arrive at what feels to be a natural tempo. Then is the time to consult my friend the metronome to determine if I am on the right track. If I have approximated the composer's tempo, I'm ready to move forward and dig deeper. If, on the other hand, I discover a dramatic dichotomy between the indicated tempo and the tempo I am feeling, then I am compelled to reconsider my thought process in an effort to reconcile the difference. The goal is always to find that sweet spot in terms of tempo that honors the composer's intent and is perceived as a natural tempo by me. That is rarely a precise tempo dictated by the metronome.

Similarly, I much prefer never to engage an ensemble in rehearsal without a metronome being readily available. With that said, I do not want the metronome to be the be-all-end-all of tempo. Instead, I view it as a guide or reference resource. In most cases the metronome on my phone is muted and calibrated to the desired tempo. I can quickly reference the appropriate musical pace if need be, but the transmission of the tempo from the conductor to the ensemble remains visual. With rare exception, I never allow the music making to be disturbed by the repetitive throb of an audible pulse. That's for individual musicians to do when they *practice* as opposed to what we do collectively when we *rehearse.*

There is one final factor to consider. One must be keenly aware of the differences in and relationships between tempo and internal rhythmic pulse. Without question, tempo is important. But it can easily be observed as a rigid, empirical, external value that is totally disenfranchised from any expressive, artistic emotion. Composer, conductor, and author Gunther Schuller emphatically stated, "I do not believe that an exacting adherence to metronomic indications will by itself guarantee a good, a great, or a 'correct' performance."[14]

On the other hand, I like to think of internal pulse as the rhythmic fiber of the music that exists within each beat. It suggests a more holistic approach that embraces, melds, and in some cases galvanizes all elements of music making into an artistic whole. It is that internal pulse that gives music unity. It is what happens inside each beat where much of the music lives. I often think of pulse as the heartbeat of the music.

INTERLUDE

THOUGHTS ON OUR MORE SUBTLE SINS

There is clearly an objective component of measurability in the sins we have discussed thus far. After all, 120 beat per minute can be viewed as exactly that: 120 beats per minute. Legato notes are measurably longer than staccato notes. Rhythms can be broken down into their smallest denominator and measured precisely. *Forte* passages must be rendered with more volume than *piano* passages. In each case there is an observable, measurable outcome that can be quantified.

Perhaps that is why we obsess over these elements of music making. They afford us an opportunity to make comparisons and check boxes. They lend themselves to convenient inclusion in a rubric, allowing us to focus on the "craft of execution," and while doing so we are freed from any accountability of making artistic decisions.

But now we transition into three sins that are far more elusive: the sins of absence of line, ignoring the function of silence, and failure to consider the role of proportion. These sins appear to be void of any objective content that would allow one to compartmentalize or objectify their substance or outcomes. Simply put, there is no real or perceived yardstick for measurability. The subtlety of these transgressions makes them difficult to analyze or describe. Yet they are at the epicenter of some of the most profound musical moments we will ever encounter or create.

It is also important to recognize that the lines between these three sins are blurred. While they can be identified and discussed independently, the truth remains that they are intimately intertwined and should be considered holistically in our music making. To do any less, well, that might be an eighth sin.

One might simply argue that these moments of musical virtues are right because they "feel right." They exist not because of what one sees on the page but rather because of the artistic, emotional connections they create. When present they have the potential to capture our musical soul. But let's be honest. That's akin to me saying, "Here is a simple way to put smoke in a box."

Instead, let's acknowledge the reality that we are the products of all we have encountered, imagined, or experienced. We have had those "goose bump moments." We like them, and we want more. So how you confront these final sins should perhaps be driven by who you are as a musical artist at the moment and what you envision your future artistry might be.

Read again the profound words of Saint Francis of Assisi:

> *He who works with his hands is a laborer.*
> *He who works with his hands and his head is a craftsman.*
> *He who works with his hands and his head and his heart*
> *is an artist.*

Now read on, letting your heart, your musical being rather than your head, enlighten your pathway.

Chapter 5

SIN #5: ABSENCE OF LINE

Music is not a bunch of separated notes strung together,
but rather one note that swims from pitch to pitch on a line.
— David McGill[15]

Fact! The art of creating musical line is core to the artistry of all that we do. It is the overriding fundamental human element found in all forms of auditory communication. The dictionary defines "line," among other things, as "direction and shape." Think about it. Can one imagine compelling oratory void of pacing, inflection, and nuance all intended to deepen the meaning and importance of the message? What would be the reaction to an actor's soliloquy if delivered word perfect in a monotone voice contour with all syllables rendered with identical weight and emotionless pacing? Certainly, the raw material would be present, but the essence of the message would be totally lost. The effect might be likened to a computer-generated electronic voice that simply regurgitates factual information, raw data, if you will. Think automated phone messages on your phone. In truth, for communication to be emotional and infused with human meaning there must be line, or nuance, if you will.

I've been told that one of the legendary Frederick Fennell's favorite mantras was, "Live for the line!" To be honest, I can't cite this account as fact, but I would like to think it was indeed true. Furthermore, even if maestro Fennell did not utter this proclamation, I would passionately argue that his music making embraced its import, and without question, its message was always in evidence each time he stepped on the podium. We should do no less.

Unfortunately, in our desire to accurately recreate the notation we see on the page and be true to the objective exactness of the composer's myriad notations, we easily fall into the trap of relegating musical line to a place of secondary importance, or tragically in some cases, no importance whatsoever. As a consequence, we play note by note and from measure to measure rather than embracing the musical phrases and organic content that are the holistic essence of musical artistry.

Let's begin by drawing some correlations with the spoken word. Actors spend countless hours determining how they will deliver their lines. Yes, there's that word "line" again! It's not about how they will pronounce the words, but rather how the delivery of the words will be sequenced and how the true meaning of what is being spoken will be revealed.

Let me give you an example. In Act I, Scene 7 of Shakespeare's *Macbeth* there is an exchange between Macbeth and Lady Macbeth as they plot to assassinate Duncan. Macbeth poses the question, "If we should fail?" Lady Macbeth responds, "We fail!" She then goes on to orchestrate the deed.

For a moment, think about how many ways she could have framed her two-word response depending on the punctuation mark that followed it. As written, her response might be a simple statement of fact, that being a plan and emphatic affirmation of that reality: We fail!

But what if she was absolutely obsessed with the deed regardless of success or consequences. Her response might then be arrogant and perhaps sneering. It would be spoken slowly and emphatically with a slight downward nuance to the end of each word.

Another possibility: What if her line were followed by a question mark? That might suggest that it had not occurred to her that failure was an option. In that case there might be a sense of surprise in her voice with the words spoken quickly with an upward, questioning tone to the word "fail," as if to say, "I never thought of that."

In each case, it is how the words are spoken and how they relate to one another that reveals their underlying meaning. It is the pacing, the line, and the emotional connection that reveals the explicit, deeper sense of what is being communicated. To my way of thinking, this is the essence of line in all forms of human communication and central to what we do in music making. This commitment to line must be present even in the simplest of melodies or in the most elemental statements of musical thought.

Let's look at more examples of line and the spoken word. What about the first three words of the Pledge of Allegiance? Spoken blandly without line or inflection they communicate little: "I pledge allegiance." But what do those three words communicate? Without line or inflection, they are raw, emotionless, and without meaning. They are just words. But state the pledge three times with emphasis and inflection on the boldfaced word in each repetition of the statement.

1. "*I* pledge allegiance."
2. "I *PLEDGE* allegiance."
3. "I pledge *ALLEGIANCE*."

Doing so completely reshapes the message. Now there is context and, in truth, dramatically different meanings. Putting the emphasis on a different word totally changes the intent or "spin," if you will, of the statement.

There is yet another option. It could be spoken in a questioning context, as if to rebut your willingness to pledge: "I? . . . pledge allegiance?"

Let's look at it another way, and this time you determine the appropriate delivery of the text. General Thomas J. Jackson acquired his nickname "Stonewall Jackson" at the Battle of Bull Run. History tells us that another general, upon seeing Jackson in battle, declared in words to the effect, "There is Jackson, standing like a stone wall!" Powerful words indeed. But there is some speculation as to the context in which these words were uttered. There is the prevailing argument that Jackson was unswerving in the face of battle and thus rallied the Virginian troops under his command. Now, in that context please pause for a moment and speak those words loudly and forcefully, confirming what that observant general was proclaiming. Do it several times, placing the emphasis on different words. But in each case make it a statement of triumph and validation of his steadfastness. You get the idea. Go ahead! No one is listening. Put yourself on the battlefield and shout it out.

But there is another historical point of view. Some say that Jackson was shell-shocked, petrified, and so in fear that he was unable to act or move. He was just "standing there." If that were the case, how would you say those same words? Your declaration would be far less compelling and perhaps laced with mockery and ridicule. Go ahead, try it again. Repeat the statement with slightly different but equally condemning nuances. Maybe there should be some sarcasm in your voice. With little effort you can spin the statement in countless ways. This, my friends, is line. It is what gives words their true meaning. It is the essence of human expression. Failing to create line in music is, you guessed it, a sin.

There are at least three roadblocks that hinder our sensitivity to line as conductors and instrumentalists, the first being that the mechanics of playing an instrument can easily be objectified. It's a matter of pushing buttons and reading rhythms while we blow, bow, or strike an instrument, often all done to the throbbing beat of a metronome. The goal is to get it correct. It's like painting by the numbers. If you follow instructions, being careful and exact, at the end of the day you have created a picture. But is that picture art? I think not.

Secondly, in the quest for technical mastery our feelings and emotions tend to be set to the side, put on hold, postponed until later, or ignored altogether. After all, most of the educational music assessments we encounter are designed to measure observable outcomes. The focus is on the right notes, the right rhythms, acceptable tone quality, attention to tuning, and the application of a broad array of ensemble skills. But what about the music?

Dr. Robert Duke, professor at University of Texas and advocate extraordinaire in music and human learning, proposes the introduction of musicianship (yes, that includes musical line) from the very beginning. For example, he suggests that the moment a young student masters a simple three- to five-note melody (we are talking beginning band or orchestra here) they should be encouraged to play it as if it were a lullaby for a younger sibling, then played again in a style that might frighten the family pet, and yet again played with a sense of sadness or joy. This simple challenge totally reframes the experience and the artistry of the outcome. Just as children use inflection and emotion in their vocabulary from the beginning, shouldn't students be encouraged to play expressively (translation: presence of line) from the very beginning? There is only one right answer to that question: YES!

Finally, and this is my personal take, there is the fact that music notation has evolved and grown exponentially over the centuries.

The original Mozart manuscript lives in the United States Library of Congress. It belongs to us! A stunning reproduction of this musical treasure is currently available from GIA Publications.

As I'm writing about this particular sin, I am holding in my hands and looking at a facsimile of the holograph of the Mozart "Gran Partita," K. 361. It is the actual manuscript score in Mozart's hand.

For me personally, turning these pages is a religious experience. After all, without doubt it is one of the landmark works written for our medium. Yet page after page there is nothing but an array of masterfully conceived notes and rhythms. Musical markings are noticeably lacking. On occasion you will find a *forte, piano,* and perhaps a *sforzando piano.* Beyond that there are a few staccato markings and hastily scribbled requests for a crescendo. (Mozart would not have gotten high marks for penmanship, by the way!) But, in truth, Mozart left the music making up to us. There is no micromanaging of every note and measure here.

Now fast-forward and look at any contemporary instrumental score regardless of difficulty level. You will see more markings on one score page than you would observe in an entire movement of the K. 361. This proliferation of musical markings, or perhaps better defined as "notation inflation," has the potential to be either a blessing or a curse.

Here is a recent example of language addressing articulation that I encountered in the preface of a 2018 score.

ARTICULATION

Not tongued

- Slurred – phrased, with shape; no tongue

Tongued

- Staccato – short value, not very stressed
- Wedge (staccatissimo) – short value; very stressed and pointed (a hybrid between accent and staccato)
  - ○ At end of slur – full value into end of slur with stress on last pitch
- None – medium value, detached; not stressed
- Marcato – medium value, detached; very stressed while rounded
- Accent – full value; strong stress in front of note
- Tenuto – full value: slight tongue, very rounded slight stress between pitches. A hybrid between legato and mild accent)
  - ○ At end of slur – hold full value into next pitch, usually the same note
  - ○ At end of tied note – reminder to hold full value into next bar
  - ○ Two or more successive tenutos between slurs – slight rounded stress on pitches while full value (like mild accents)

Of course, this level of detail gives us a more precise picture of the composer's intent, and perhaps in many contemporary scores it is desirable, if not essential. But there is also the danger that, at times, this abundance of objective information gets in the way of the actual music. I would argue that we can easily get so involved in observing and applying the myriad musical markings that fill the page that we fail to think about how the music really goes. We are just progressing from note to note and measure to measure checking off a never-ending array of dynamics, articulation markings, and performance instructions. Musical line is simply not on our musical radar screen.

So, how do we chart a pathway out of this conundrum? After all, there is no list of rules, no Ten Commandments of musical line, no dos and don'ts to guide us. The challenge is complicated by the fact that, in truth, with the plethora of shapes and symbols that come under the heading of musical notation there are actually no markings for human emotions or feelings. We are left to our own intellect, human experiences, and musical intuitiveness to figure it out. But there is hope. There are some guideposts we can apply to minimize and buffer our sin. First and foremost...

Make music from the beginning. As Daniel Barenboim eloquently stated, "When the technical problems of finger dexterity have been solved, it is too late to add musicality, phrasing and musical expression. That is why I never practise mechanically. . . . If we work mechanically, we run the risk of changing the very nature of the music."[16] His words challenge us to always make musicality our central focus. There must be musical meaning from the beginning. Even if there are technical obstacles to overcome, these challenges must not be isolated from our ultimate vision for musical expressiveness.

Thus, if you study a score, engage in practice, or navigate a rehearsal with no reflection or contemplation as to the musical intent of the notes on the page, you have committed one of the greatest of musical transgressions. It is the sin of pursuing craft void of an awareness of the musical intent or the artistry it represents.

Explore dynamic inflection that is not marked in the score. Let me quickly say that dynamic inflection goes far beyond the related but broader consideration of dynamic contrast and the correlation between the almost limitless spectrum of louds and softs. That is another sin discussed elsewhere.

Let's not forget that James Boyk, pianist, teacher, and author, states that "dynamic inflection refers to the natural rise and fall of volume in any communicative sound." He goes on to say that "a musical phrase may be marked *forte* (loud) in the score. That does not mean that all notes of the phrase are equally loud. Rather, there's an expressive moment-to-moment flexibility to them."[17] This rise and fall of dynamics is one of the essential qualities of creating musical line.

This ebb and flow of dynamics is essential if we are to capture the human element and emotional content of any expressive musical phrase. With rare exception, it is difficult, if not impossible, to create musical line without dynamic contrast. And as discussed in a previous chapter, it can't be the dynamic contrast you think you are creating, but rather the dynamic contrast that is perceived by the listener that truly matters. It is that emotional connection between the performer and the listener where the artistry of the music comes alive.

When appropriate, allow room for an element of rhythmic inexactness to be present in the creation of musical line. While this sin is discussed in greater detail elsewhere, it plays a pivotal role in the creation of line and must be referenced here as well. Certainly, there are times that rhythmic exactness is crucial, but there will always be those occasions where a flux in tempo and pulse enriches and deepens the musical communication even though there is no indication in the score for such variation to occur. I've said it before and I will say it again: Color outside the lines.

These subtle rhythmic and tempo irregularities have the potential to enrich the character of the musical line, much like the natural flaws in leather, granite, marble, or wood add richness and beauty. To put it another way, give the music rhythmic freedom to embrace human, emotional expressiveness.

Be mindful that harmony helps define the line. Obviously, the melodic contour of the music reveals much regarding options for how the musical line might unfold, but never forget that the harmonic content can and should influence the artistry of our journey as well. It remains one of the composer's most powerful and evocative devices. The harmony can offer direction, create drama, and reveal musical inevitability. It can give momentum, enlighten the musical pathway, inject elements of surprise, and/or define places of rest. Above all, it serves to guide, support, and underscore the musical journey.

It is essential that we listen to the harmony with our hearts. In all of its guises it remains one of music's most powerful, eloquent adornments. Harmonies can be simple and straightforward, and at other times, compelling and immensely complex. It is sometimes subtle, hovering just below the surface of the music, other times proclaimed equally intertwined with other musical elements or, on occasion, vigorously flaunted as a centerpiece of a musical moment. Our charge? To look for opportunities to bring harmony to the fore and allow it to be a beacon that highlights and underscores the music's pathway.

> Harmony alone can stir the emotions. It is the one source from which melody directly emanates and draws its power.
>
> — Jean-Philippe Rameau (1683–1764)

Accompaniment (secondary parts) can create continuity and also help extend the line. Always be on the lookout for places in the music where the accompaniment actually enhances the primary music. Composers do so often, especially in slow, sustained lines. Here are the first seven measures of the fifth movement of *Divertimento* by Vincent Persichetti. The musical focus is a haunting B-flat cornet solo accompanied by a small chamber ensemble of woodwinds and brass.

Notice that with a few exceptions the accompaniment moves while the solo sustains, and the accompaniment sustains while the cornet soloist moves. Also note that there is some melodic or harmonic movement on every count. The line flows from beat to beat and measure to measure without interruption. The combined efforts of soloist and accompaniment unify to create an arching phrase embracing the first seven measures of the movement. Every note and its relationship to the notes that surround it are crucial. The underlying musical line cannot be achieved by simply counting beats and playing at the same time. There must be an interconnection with all that unfolds. The more intertwined and connected the individual parts become, the more unified and organic the music will sound.

In this kind of music, I often ask the soloist to play the solo line while those with the accompaniment simply listen. Then I ask the accompaniment to fit their parts "inside" the solo line as opposed to just counting the rhythms as they plod from beat to beat. And remember here what Casals said about music being "a succession of rainbows."

Divertimento, Mvt. 5 "Soliloquy," mm. 1–7, reduced score in C

*There is potential for the "white" notes to sustain the line and
the "black" notes to connect the music, resulting in musical line.*
Thank about it. Particularly in lyrical music there is often a vital
interplay between the "white" notes and the "black" notes. The
black notes roam to and fro as they provide movement, melodic
interest, and tell the story. Simultaneously, the white notes serve to
anchor, support, and sustain the music, sometimes even creating
moments of reflection. Both elements play an essential role, and
it is our awareness of this interplay that brings the music to life.
The black notes can't just be rhythmically accurate, and the white
notes can't just sit there if we expect there to be musical line and
direction. And remember that dynamics can be used to give white
notes personality and direction. It is essential that we find and
reveal the musical journey that is in the score.

Music making must be more than problem solving. I fear that because we as music educators function in an academic setting and consequently tend to treat music making like any other academic enterprise, we view it as an equation or a problem to solve. We are seeking a measured outcome. Thus, we easily become obsessed with seeking and being satisfied with the "correct answer."

Music, unlike art, sculpture, or theater, is the one art that you can't experience visually. And never forget, the score alone can make no sound. It must be felt. We are the music makers, and our musical utterances must be heartfelt as opposed to an objective recreation of the notes on the page.

In summary, line is the seamless aural representation of all that we see on the printed page, not just the raw data of notes and rhythms or the correctness of the notation, but rather the *feeling* of the music. It is what we hear and feel when the bar lines go away. Musical line is the culmination and ultimate manifestation of sinless music making.

CHAPTER 6

SIN #6: IGNORNING THE FUNCTION OF SILENCE IN MUSIC

*Music and silence combine strongly because
music is done with silence, and silence is full of music.*
— Marcel Marceau

Silence! What exactly is it? In some contexts, it can be defined simply as "forbearance from speech or noise" or "absence of sound or noise." But such definitions can be woefully inadequate, particularly when it comes to describing the powerful role that silence plays in the world of music.

British conductor and author Paul Hillier perhaps said it best when he observed,

> All music emerges from silence, to which sooner or later it must return. At its simplest we may conceive of music as the relationship between sounds and the silence that surrounds them. Yet silence is an imaginary state in which all sounds are absent, akin perhaps to the infinity of time and space that surrounds us. We cannot ever hear utter silence, nor can we fully imagine such concepts as infinity and eternity. When we create music, we express life. But the source of music is silence, which is the ground of our

musical being, the fundamental note of life. How we live depends on our relationship with death; how we make music depends on our relationship with silence.[18]

It is my personal belief that silence gives music context in countless ways. The presence of silence creates drama. Silence precedes all music making and it is the ultimate resting place of all music once sounded. In addition, silence punctuates the ebb and flow of the music, remaining an ever-present force available to create moments of anticipation for what is yet to come, to serve as an instant of reflection on what has just passed, or perhaps to intensify the emotional message of the music unfolding. Furthermore, one might say there is the potential for silence to create a border for the music, much as a tasteful frame might surround and highlight an artful painting. It is an integral part of the DNA of music making and, as such, it behooves us to remain mindful of the intimate relationship between sound and silence that is encapsulated in the score.

So, what do all these abstract, perhaps even esoteric, thoughts about silence have to do with our day-to-day music making in our rehearsal halls and classrooms? After all, our hands go up, our hands come down, and the music starts. Then one of our goals, among many, is to make sure that no one plays on the rests and that we all stop together at the end of the final measure so that unified silence is achieved. We have notes, rhythms, and tuning to deal with, all in the context of refining tone quality, balance, and blend. So, how can those moments where there is no sound be so important and so worthy of our thoughtful reflection?

Consider, if you will, that infamous line heard in those dreaded infomercials. The product "you can't do without" is described in detail, and then we hear the salesman proclaim, "But wait . . .

there's more!" You know the rest! In this case I would suggest that for our discussion, the "more" is the silence. I contend that we should be as concerned about the silence and its significance in our music making as we are about the role that notes and rhythms play. Sound and silence are forever intertwined, and the relationship between the two must be factored into all musical decisions. Failing to do so is a misdeed.

As one ponders silence, countless variable imaginary images emerge. What should the atmosphere be before the music begins? Are those rests in the music simply a break in the action, a relief point for the clarinets to breathe, or is there a deeper, more artistic meaning in the score just waiting to be revealed? Perhaps the rests can be a part of the musical line. Do they create atmosphere, drama, context, or contrast? What should be the mood, energy level, and sense of closure as the music ends? If music indeed emerges from silence, travels over silence, and ultimately returns to silence, then perhaps there is undeniable logic associated with the contemplation of the silence that surrounds the music. In truth, the factors to consider are endless.

> For musicians, silence is the soil into which we have to plant music; we must nourish the soil, make sure it's of good quality so that our seeds will take root.
>
> — Stephen Hough, concert pianist, in "Why Musicians Need Silence in an Always-Connected World"

To begin with, let's face it: We live in a noisy world, our music world included. Your rehearsal hall is anything but a quiet place. Bells ring, announcements are made, students enter, students exit, mutes are dropped, percussion instruments are moved, and, often, the metronome throbs. Any and all of these audible interruptions are arguably inevitable, but certainly the potential exists to minimize such intrusions if we accept the challenge to nurture a culture of silence that gives us the freedom and luxury of creating music as it was intended, that being a canvas of compelling silence on which we display our music making.

Let's look at this premise another way. When do people listen the most intently? Is it in a room filled with noise? Is it in a world of acoustical clutter? In such environments our ears simply default to the most obvious sound source available, or we opt to listen generically or not at all. Our sensitivity is blurred by the cacophony of sonic discord that surrounds us. In a worst-case scenario we are tempted to tune out all sound and listen to nothing. I would argue that it is only when there is an approximation of absolute silence that we truly enlist our highest level of listening skills.

THE SILENCE THAT PRECEDES THE MUSIC

Juilliard composer, author, and teacher Bruce Adolphe says that before any sound there is already meaning. Therefore, the first notes we hear must be "in character." There must be context to the music that is about to unfold. Two realities are essential. First, there must be what Frederick Fennell called "convincing silence." An artistic environment is essential. Secondly, the conductor must be in his or her musical center and connected to the music before it ever makes a sound. Only then can the beginning of the work at hand begin with compelling musical intent. Some might say that this is a sophisticated concept reserved for the refined artist, but I would argue that it is an essential necessity. And I assure you that young students can "get it."

> A musician plays through the silence.
>
> — Bruce Adolphe in *What to Listen for in the World* (p. 26)

Does the music gently emerge from silence? Does it leap onto the sonic stage? Does it "bite," or is there an air of subtlety as the character of the music emerges? The options are limitless. All that is required is that there is a point of view before there is sound. Simply starting together is not enough.

There is also that moment of silence when the conductor becomes one with the music that is about to unfold. There is a captivating manifestation of that moment of silence in a TED Talk first posted on June 8, 2011. The presenter is maestro Carl St. Clair, who has served as conductor of the Pacific Symphony for more than twenty-five years. The focus of the talk is the issue of what conductors bring to the podium through thoughtful study and reflection. In the final demonstration, which beautifully exhibited the deepest level of artful reflection, there is a magic moment. Maestro St. Clair returns to the podium, where one can observe a dramatic, inward moment of quiet pause as he reaches his musical center. Then, and only then, does he initiate his artful collaboration with the musicians.

I encourage you to observe this powerful moment and give thought to what it represents. You will find it at the 11:30 mark of this video: https://www.youtube.com/watch?v=ezVequnPmUc

Certainly, Carl St. Clair is a world-renowned conductor who lives in a world filled with artistry. Thus, it is easy to argue this isn't what we do. After all, we are music educators, band directors, or whatever label we choose to assign ourselves. This isn't necessary for us to aspire to this high level of artistic engagement. I wholeheartedly disagree. I respectfully contend that each one of us must strive to emulate this level of artistry each time we stand before our students. To do any less deprives our students of the very best that is within us and the very best that music has to offer them.

THE SEVEN DEADLY SINS OF MUSIC MAKING · RICHARD FLOYD

For many, this mindset can be an acquired skill. Let's make an analogy with yoga. "Yoga" is the Sanskrit word for union. In its simplest context, yoga uses breathing techniques, exercise, and meditation in an effort to improve health and happiness. It must be practiced. Perhaps there is a correlation here. What we are seeking is a union between sound (insert the word "music") and silence. How we achieve it can be a very personal journey, but it is a journey that is a requisite for each of us. Without an awareness of and a relationship with silence, there is no context for music making.

THE SILENCE THAT ACCOMPANIES THE MUSIC

Some forty years ago I had the good fortune to attend a lecture at Yale University focusing on the Mozart Serenades for Winds given by the great oboist Robert Bloom. He was at the peak of his career. It was life changing. I was amazed that he talked as much about the rests as he did the notes. He insisted that rests must be "energy-filled silence." His words remain with me to this day. It has been my experience that for that to happen the rests must exist in the context of being "silent notes." Thus, a seamless connection is created. The silence becomes a compelling part of the phrase and plays a vital role in the musical line.

Lesley Sisterhen McAllister, professor of piano at Baylor University, proclaims in her book *The Balanced Musician: Integrating Mind and Body for Peak Performance* that "rests give music life." She goes on to state that rests "provide a respite from tense moments, add suspense, or provide clear breaks between phrases or sections."[19] None of that emotion is fathomable unless we contemplate it and factor its reality into our music making. In simplest terms, music needs silence in order to be fully understood and appreciated by the listener.

In the book *Casals and the Art of Interpretation*, author David Blum speaks of what Casals called "the art of the rest." He states that Casals counseled performers "not to seek to minimize the effect of a rest" but to instead "grant it its full due. If the line of feeling remains unbroken the silences will take on expressive intensity."[20] Blum goes on to say that such moments have the potential to be spellbinding.

> The silences are also music.
>
> — Pablo Casals, as quoted in David Blum's *Casals and the Art of Interpretation* (p. 98)

Let's explore examples of this eternal truth and consider how one might add depth and meaning to the music by considering the function of silence.

At a recent music conference, I attended an inspiring session featuring the combined talent and artistry of composer Eric Whitacre and the former director of bands at the University of Miami, Gary Green. The focus of the session was a discussion of Whitacre's band adaptation of *Lux Aurumque*. This is a piece I have conducted countless times and always with a reverent, perhaps even sacred, approach to the profound role that silence seems to play in many of the measures. Personally, I have never been able to view these rests as being rhythmic or precise. To me, they simply hover just below the threshold of sound, drawing their beauty from the impreciseness of their duration. For example, in the opening eight measures, the music on beat three of measures 2, 4, 6, and 8 simply evaporates somewhere in the afterglow of the fourth count. There is no rhythmic release. The music is "beatless." (And I might add that I view the rests as being void of time in the strictest sense of the word.)

Lux Aurumque, mm. 1–8

I sometimes thought I was perhaps overthinking this element of the music or in danger of exercising too much artistic license; that is until I heard Eric Whitacre's revealing comments. He offered persuasive validation for my rationale. First, *Lux Aurumque* began as a choral work. The premiere of the piece was intended to take place in a cathedral known for its extended reverb. In such a venue, the fourth count rest would be almost non-existent, as the last vocal sounds uttered at the conclusion of beat three would still be reverberating as the next measure began. With the help of the hall, the music would become near seamless. The rests would be embraced in the music. Consider, by contrast, a band performing this piece in a typical concert hall with the rests precisely timed (perhaps, God forbid, by the accuracy of a metronome). The music becomes segmented and disjunct. The magic is lost. And, yes, we have erred.

Whitacre made yet another observation. He said that he envisioned that these opening two-bar phrases would create the illusion of inhaling for four counts and exhaling for four counts, resulting in a flowing, organic sensation. The impreciseness of the act becomes the core of its natural beauty and makes a powerful human connection for the performers. While the notation on paper appears blunt and precise, the final results must reflect the humanness of the music.

Does every rest require this level of thought and reflection? Perhaps not. After all, some rests are just that: rests. They punctuate the music. In those cases, they simply have a functional, perhaps pragmatic role to play. But the possibility of this level of contemplation must always be in the back of one's mind as such musical decisions are made. To do any less is a transgression!

A small, seemingly insignificant rest can have an equally artistic role. Consider the expressive qualities of the flute melody (doubled in the trumpet) at Letter B in John Mackey's *Sheltering Sky*. The overarching line can easily be broken by the overstatement of the eighth note rest on the "and" of four in the second measure. If that measure is approached with absolute rhythmic precision and carefully metered, the result is likely to be a precise release of the E-flat at the end of the measure. The music dies and there is no connection with the four measures to follow. But the musical effect is totally different if the length of the dotted quarter note is slightly extended and there is no diminishment of dynamics. There is a sense of connection with the music that follows, and the rest essentially becomes a pick-up or a bridge, if you will, to the beginning of the next measure. The rest then becomes a seamless connection with what is to follow. In other words, the emphasis must be on the end of the sounded E-flat as opposed to the rhythmic exactness of the rest that follows. These two elements exist to enhance one another and extend the musical thought for the full duration of the extended phrase.

Sheltering Sky

Is there a pragmatic strategy that applies and helps ensure a sustained line? I would argue yes. Never forget that most students first and foremost view a rest as an opportunity to take a breath. This can be true even during a rest with a duration of less than one beat. Students perceive the rest to be a license to take a gulp of air. Do not be deceived. These small rests do not imply a stop or pause in the music making. They should be viewed more as a punctuation mark. We don't breathe with the insertion of every comma, at the end of a line of prose, or at the end of every sentence we communicate verbally, so why are we compelled to breathe every time a brief moment of silence is inserted in the music?

I would propose that this phrase be viewed as being without interruption, with the eighth rest being an integral part of the line. The rest should not imply the conscious act of stopping the music completely and then restarting after the rest is completed. Far from it. The logical, natural solution is that no one breathes on the rest.

If similar phrases are so long that they can't be played in one breath, then ask players to stagger breathe so the line is continuous and, again, no one breathes on the eighth note rest. The musical message takes on a more holistic persona, and the rest is now a part of the music.

Similar examples can be found in faster tempo, highly rhythmic musical examples. Here is the flute/piccolo/xylophone line found at measure 97 in Frank Ticheli's *Dancing on Water*.

Dancing on Water, mm. 97–100

At first glance it appears to be a series of unrelated rhythmic fragments each lasting a measure or less. In truth, the sequence can be played that way and viewed to be correct. In such cases, wind players will tend to accentuate the first eighth note of each fragment and back away from the final eighth note before each rest, thus reinforcing the notion that it is nothing more than a series of disjunct fragments. The energy and drive of the music into the silence that connects with the next note grouping is lost.

Look at it another way. Remember Robert Shaw's words in our discussion of dynamics: "The dynamics never sit. They are always in motion." What if the musicians were encouraged to give a slight crescendo to each rhythmic fragment, thus creating the illusion of momentum and a sense of musical connection with the rest that follows each fragment? The final eighth note then sounds more like a pick-up note to silence. A musical connection emerges with each fragment being fused to the next to create an extended rhythmic overlay to the lyrical, soaring line heard in the lower voices while serving as a preamble to the oboe solo beginning in measure 105. The oboe solo must respond in kind and unfold with a sense of unity as opposed to sounding like five disjunct fragments. Treating these eighth rests as "energy-filled silence" gives assurance that there will be a musical connection, a seamless musical gesture and not simply a series of abstract rhythmic slivers.

Finally, remember in these kinds of musical statements there is a significant difference in how a rest sounds when executed on a wind instrument as opposed to a string instrument. On the page they may look the same, but in the case of string instruments the sound continues. There is "afterglow" that gives the tone length and resonance even though the bow has left the string. To achieve that same lyrical connection with the silence, wind players must use the air (their breath) to give the note more life, length, and energy. Only then do the rests become a part of the music.

THE SILENCE THAT FOLLOWS THE MUSIC

As previously stated, all music returns to silence. It is inevitable. But how? Does the music just stop? Does it go reluctantly? Or does it rush to embrace silence? Is it obvious? Should it be subtle? The options are limitless.

In some contexts, I consider the notion that the music doesn't actually stop. Perhaps it simply evaporates. It's like blowing out a candle and watching the last whiff of smoke go away. Examples of pieces where this might be the desired closure include Balmages's *Rippling Watercolors*, Grainger's *Irish Tune from County Derry*, the last movement of de Meij's *Lord of The Rings*, or Whitacre's *Sleep*.

Now to be sure there are some pragmatic risks associated with this sublime musical gesture. What if the tone loses resonance as it morphs into silence? What if there is a failure of the ensemble to release the final note uniformly? Undesirable things can happen. In truth, there is a fine line between coaxing a beautiful sound gently into silence and having the result become an untidy release void of artistry.

There is an essential musical element that comes into play here, which I refer to as the "threshold of sonority." It is the point of ensemble tone quality at which playing softer (or louder) results in a distortion of tonal beauty. That threshold is unique to each ensemble and is dependent on countless factors of tone quality, resonance, intensity, and, of course, musical maturity. Be assured every assembly of musicians has one, and it is essential that we first identify it and, second, that we make a conscious effort to extend it as we explore an ever-expanding palette of dynamic contrast. But one cannot find that magic balance without some trial and error coupled with a focused collaboration between conductor and musicians. Is it worth it? Absolutely! So, when it seems appropriate, don't hesitate to go for it!

There is a great story about a performance of Mahler's Ninth Symphony with the San Francisco Symphony. The performance of the full symphony easily exceeded an hour. After multiple, glorious, overpowering musical moments, the ending involved only second violins and violas. The last note simply disappeared into overwhelming silence. But the musicians and the conductor remained frozen. In truth, the conductor, without gesture, was still conducting. The music continued. One might say that the conductor had not stopped conducting but rather was intimately holding the silence. No one dared applaud. The silence served to extend the music making and enrich the rapture of the moment. Finally, the conductor lowered his arms. Then, and only then, was the music over.

On the other hand, there are other cases where the music actually collides with the silence. The closure is abrupt and instantaneous. The powerful "open fifth" conclusion to the second movement of *Spangled Heavens* by Donald Grantham is a graphic example of this approach. It is immediate and abrupt. The power of the silence that follows is overpowering and filled with drama. It beautifully sets up the light-hearted beginning of the following movement. A generic release would be musically unsatisfying. A tapered release would fail to capture the musical intent. Other examples of this abrupt leap into silence would include the magnificent E-flat major chord concluding the first movement of the Holst *First Suite in E-flat* or the monolithic closure found in the final movement of *Lincolnshire Posy*.

Between these two extremes are countless subtle variations. Your musical intuition and vision will dictate where you land on this scale of returning to silence. The bottom line is that the end of such a note must mean something other than a clean release. All that matters is that you make a personal, artistic, musical decision about that magic moment when sound reenters the silence from which it came.

> The right word may be effective, but no word was ever as effective as a rightly timed pause.
>
> — Mark Twain

CAVEAT

With all that said, obvious silence is not always a good thing. While one must be cognizant of the artistic, essential role of silence, there remains the reality that unwanted silence can and does occur.

Examine the woodwind accompaniment at the trio of *Sea Songs* by Ralph Vaughan Williams. It is a fluent eighth note line that follows the harmonic scheme of the music and supports the flowing melody sounded in the lower voices of the ensemble. Eighth note rests punctuate each measure of this accompaniment. Unfortunately, the tendency for players is to clip the last eighth note of each note grouping as if it had a staccato marking. The result is a repetitive, gaping silence that is contrary to the musical intent. There is too much silence, and the line becomes disjunct. The intended musical outcome must be a long flowing line with the rests playing the role of a silent connection to the next pattern. In this case, too much silence is a deficiency.

Sea Songs

Yet another example of this actuality is found in the masterful transcription by William E. Rhoads of Charles Ives's *Variation on "America."* In several instances the entire band arrives on a C major chord on beat two of the measure, and all have a quarter note rest on beat three. William Rhoads was wise. He knew that bands would tend to abbreviate the length of the quarter note on beat two, leaving an extended silence on beat three. His solution? A tie to silence that reminds the conductor and players to resist the temptation of brevity and to carry that beat two C major chord all the way to the third count. It also suggests to me that the volume should be sustained for the full duration of the note. Not all composers and arrangers are so detailed. Thus, it becomes our job to fill in the blanks.

Variations on "America"

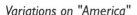

Let's consider one final example. In the second movement at Letter C of *Suite Provençale* by Jan Van der Roost, there is a tender transition between the woodwind/euphonium/tuba that release at the end of beat two and the brass choir of trumpet/horn/trombone that picks up the line on beat three. In order for that connection to be compelling, the woodwind/euphonium/tuba must carry their last note all the way to beat three. The release must "touch" the third count, and the trumpet/bells must commit to a gentle but precise rhythmic entrance that bonds the connection. The result should simply be a change of sonority, a color change, if you will, that is seamless. If the release is premature and/or the entrance is late, the result will be unwanted silence and the musical connection is lost.

> Silence can stand as the softest kind of music.
>
> — Nicky Losseff and Jenny Doctor in *Silence, Music, Silent Music* (p. 2)

The musical world is filled with examples of the reality that silence comes in many guises. It plays countless roles. Only through our awareness of the function of silence can its ultimate expressiveness be achieved. Thus, it remains our challenge to make sure that the silence is proportional and in context. Nothing less will suffice.

CHAPTER 7

SIN #7: FAILURE TO CONSIDER THE ROLE OF PROPORTION

Proportion is the heart of beauty.
— Ken Follett

O h my! Where to begin? There is so much already on our plate as we consider the myriad aspects of music making. And certainly, in the six sins we have already addressed there could be multiple subsets of considerations to ponder. Where does it stop? In the words of Stephen Sondheim and James Lapine from their musical theater masterpiece *Sunday in the Park with George*, "Art isn't easy!"

Allow me to place one more essential challenge on the table, that being a consideration of the role of proportion. In simplest terms, proportion can be viewed as the relative size of parts within a whole—a musical necessity that embraces, but is not necessarily limited to, scale or symmetry. Basically, any and all things music ultimately evolve into some kind of relationship that seeks to achieve both contrast and unity. Let me immediately affirm that there is an abundance of subjectivity here, but at the end of the day it boils down to a quest for the harmonious relation of parts to each other and the relation of the collective parts to the whole.

Let's begin with the supposition that there is proportion imbedded in any musical score worthy of performance. Even a simple ABA overture or other work for young ensembles has the potential to contain some degree of proportion. It can be obvious, subtle, or hidden in the fabric of the music just waiting to be discovered.

Then, we as conductors must in turn make conscious decisions about how the elements of music such as tempo, dynamics, articulation, pacing, nuance, and so on define, bring to life, and underscore the musical proportions on the printed page. We become an indispensable part of the process. And yes, it is a joyful role that we play.

It seems appropriate to begin this conversation with a subject far more universal and far-reaching than just our beautiful world of music. That subject has to do with a fundamental, recurring mathematical relationship that can be observed all around us in nature, architecture, visual art, and music. Does that suggest that it is present in all that we proclaim as art? Absolutely not. But it is so embedded in the human experience that it becomes a very cogent place to begin. The Greeks referred to it as the Golden Ratio, and it was later known as the Divine Proportion. Regardless of the name, it is closely aligned with the Fibonacci sequence (more about that shortly). We might even think of it as an algorithm of nature.

In pure mathematical numbers it looks like this:

$$\frac{a+b}{a} = \frac{a}{b} \approx 1.618$$

It also can be displayed like this:

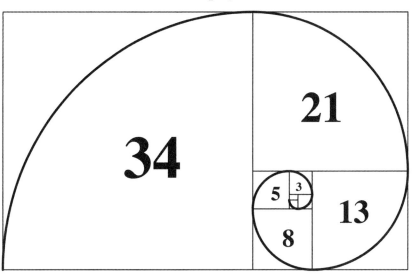

Examples abound in nature:

In visual art:

In architecture:

In graphic examples of proportion:

There is also a very close correlation with the Fibonacci sequence here. Leonardo Pisano Bigollo, better known as Fibonacci (a name given to him in the nineteenth century), was an Italian mathematician who was viewed as one of the most gifted Western world mathematicians of the Middle Ages. The Fibonacci sequence he introduced is one of the most famous formulas in mathematics. The computations create a spiraling sequence of numbers that looks like this:

0, 1, 1, 2, 3, 5, 8, 13, 21, 34, 55, 89, 144 . . .

Note that each number is the sum of the preceding two numbers. And if you divide any number by the smaller number that precedes it, the result will consistently be an approximation of 1.6180339887 . . . , which is referred to mathematically as Phi. What is Phi? If you haven't guessed, it is the basis for the Golden Ratio. Thus, there is overwhelming evidence that this sequence, these proportions, and the resulting relationships are omnipresent in our lives, our world, and indeed the greater universe. One might even be bold enough to surmise that humankind is hardwired to embrace this phenomenon.

So, what does this all have to do with music? Actually, a great deal! To be honest, music is full of these "Phi moments." Those occurrences, encounters, and experiences that resonate the most deeply with us have some kind of comfortable symmetry or proportion that gratifies the human experience. The final results are reassuring and feel satisfying.

Does this imply that only music that conforms to the properties of the Golden Ratio is great music? I hardy think so. But there is the presence of something in the natural order of things that draws each of us, to some degree, to these natural proportions. They just feel right. If we accept this premise, then proportion becomes a paramount priority for many of our artistic musical decisions.

Let me quickly dispel the notion that composers consciously ponder the Golden Ratio or the Fibonacci sequence as they undertake the creation of a new work. It has been my experience that this is rarely the case. But it is possible to trace the influence of this phenomenon of nature back to the music of Mozart, then Beethoven, and later Béla Bartók, among others. In addition, there is evidence of such "Phi moments" in today's popular music as well.

Familiar musical examples in the wind band medium that approximate the Golden Ratio would include:

Amazing Grace	Ticheli
Down a Country Lane	Copland/Patterson
Hymn to a Blue Hour	Mackey
Irish Tune from County Derry	Grainger
Lullaby to the Moon	Balmages
October	Whitacre
O Magnum Mysterium	Lauridsen
Prelude, Opus 31, No. 14	Shostakovich/Reynolds
Rippling Watercolors	Balmages
Sheltering Sky	Mackey
Shenandoah	Ticheli
Sleep	Whitacre

The following are two direct quotes from the comments section of a YouTube video for one of the above pieces. They go like this:

"I would kill to play this song again. The rush and anticipation of getting to the climax of the song. Then the relief after getting there and calming down! What an amazing song to make me feel that way."

"I want to cry over how beautiful this is when we play it at school."

Aren't those the kinds of experiences and/or sensations that we want for our students? Isn't that the "I can't live without it" reality that we all seek? It is one of the principal reasons we do what we do.

Evidence of the Golden Ratio and Fibonacci sequence is not limited to musical form and structure. It can be found in multiple other musical contexts as well. For example, there is clear evidence of the Fibonacci sequence present in the ratio between note intervals. I will leave that one to the mathematicians and instead focus on the more subtle, subjective, and interpretive considerations of proportion that reside outside the scope of the mathematical symmetry just discussed.

So, hopefully having made my case, let's set the Golden Ratio and Fibonacci sequence aside. Be assured, there remain countless circumstances where proportion and relationships become of paramount importance in our music making. How much dynamic inflection is required to create a satisfying and proportional contrast in volume of sound? Are all crescendos uniform, or might there be occasions where the crescendo is "back loaded" so there is a burst of extra volume before the arrival point? Should proportion be a factor in the pacing of an accelerando? In a case where there are two or more fermatas in a row, will they be equal length? Should they be? The list and options are limitless.

Let's start with one very specific, dynamic example of proportion and relationships in tempo, the classic *Variations on a Korean Folk Song* by John Barnes Chance. The tempo scheme is as follows.

Beginning	Con moto	Quarter Note = 96 BPM
Variation 1	Vivace	Quarter Note = 132 BPM
Variation 2	Larghetto	Quarter Note = 72 BPM
Variation 3	Allegro con brio	Quarter Note = 144 BPM
Variation 4	Sostenuto	Dotted Half Note = Half Note = 72 BPM
Finale	Con Islancio	Quarter Note = Quarter Note = 144 BPM

There is yet one more surprise. At measure 223, the brass sound the theme in augmentation at exactly one-third of the quarter note = 144 BPM tempo requested at measure 199. The melody now unfolds at a tempo of dotted half note = 48 BPM. The *pièce de résistance*? If all tempi are negotiated properly, the final statement of the theme in augmentation will be precisely at one-half the tempo of the opening. How cool is that?

I can't fathom the notion that this happened by accident or happenstance. I am convinced that this was a conscious process on the part of the composer and that these tempo markings (all multiples of twelve, by the way) are a beautiful and captivating example of how proportion can play a compelling and arguably essential role in our music making.

Let's look at another illustration of where proportion becomes a factor of consequence. On occasion a composer will indicate two or more notes in a row that are each accompanied by a fermata. When that occurs, should they be played with equal length or could there be some kind of proportional relationship between the held notes? Look no further than the last three notes of Percy Aldridge Grainger's *Irish Tune from County Derry* for an example. The last two quarter notes in the next-to-last measure are marked with fermatas for all performers, as is the whole note F major chord in the final measure. This poignant ending is often heard with the two quarter notes held for an approximately identical length, and the final whole note is held roughly four metered counts at the established tempo. The result is so predictable and unfulfilling.

There is certainly a sense of resolution and closure, but could there be a deeper, more meaningful rendition? In measure 60 the score tells us to SLOW OFF LOTS. To me this interpretive guidepost implies a proportional extension of the length of each beat as opposed to simply waiting to play three long notes at the end. If this approach is followed to its artistic conclusion, each beat is elongated in relation to the preceding note, and the fermata on beat four of measure 63 should be longer than the fermata on beat three, and the final whole note should be extended well beyond the duration of four counts. Because of the *ppp* at the end of the final measure the term *niente* immediately comes to mind. This approach offers a proportional, sequential relationship between all notes in this final phrase and results in a more satisfying sense of closure.

Going one step further, consider that the three final words in the text are "come to me." How fitting for there to be a relationship between the words that might be visually represented as follows:

come . . . toooo . . . meeeeeee

Then if we factor in the dynamic markings, the visualization might look like this:

come . . . toooo . . . meeeeeee

What about proportion in the case of a passage marked *accelerando*? Larry Daehn's wind band setting of Grainger's *Themes from "Green Bushes"* offers us a prime example of tempo relationships in regards to proportion. The editor's tempo requests are:

- A beginning tempo of Moderately Brisk, dotted half note = 66–72 BPM.
- Measure 161 marks the beginning of an accelerando.
- At measure 177, a new tempo of dotted half note = about 80 BPM is established.
- Measure 225 indicates Slightly Faster Still with the dotted half note = about 96 BPM.

To me there are two issues here to contemplate, the first being the marked tempos. What if you feel the beginning slightly faster than 72 BPM? What if, for you, this opening statement lives closer to 80 BPM? You certainly have artistic license to do so, but if that is your decision then what happens to the later tempos? I would propose that you must adjust them accordingly so that the tempo relationship is maintained for the duration of the piece. The proportional intent must be a gradual increase in tempo that ends in reckless abandon in the final eight measures.

A second consideration is the accelerando between measures 161 and 177. Think how often we hear an accelerando that is overly controlled, cautious, and perhaps restrained. Then as it reaches the arrival point, there is an abrupt leap to the new faster tempo. Certainly, there is no harm done, but is that as musically satisfying as a carefully paced, calculated accelerando that flows seamlessly into the new tempo? I think not.

So, what about the musical antithesis of the accelerando just discussed, that being a dramatic *subito ritard* leading to a new section of music? Such a moment is present in *A Movement for Rosa* by Mark Camphouse. At measure 153, the time signature changes to 9/8 with the rhythmic pattern being 3+2+2+2 at a tempo of quarter note = 160 BPM. The descriptive adverb "urgently" appears at the top of the score. This pattern and momentum continues for four measures and then abruptly transitions to 2+2+2+3 with the declaration *subito molto allargando*. It is also accompanied with the musical terms *molto sost.* and *ten.* on the final dotted eighth note. There appear to be a lot of moving parts here.

In the words of the composer, "In measure 157 I do not apply the brakes gently." Furthermore, in measure 157, "I prefer to subdivide the first six eighth notes to achieve the subito effect and then conduct three beats against the two dotted eighth notes." Regardless of how one conducts it there must be consideration of the proportion, in this case the relationship between the sequence of rhythms and note values. The musical effect should be to create the most monolithic dramatic arrival possible at measure 158.

A Movement for Rosa, mm. 153–158, score in C

There are other issues of proportion to consider here as well. The composer states that there are two distinct climaxes in the piece, the first being a dynamic low brass climax that occurs in measure 176. It is marked *fortississimo* and accompanied with the directives *molto sonoramente* and *molto allargando*. (A sidebar here: Camphouse rarely uses the *fortississimo* dynamic marking. Translation: There is a big deal here.) But if proportion is not considered in the pacing of the dynamic contrast, it would be easy to overstate the *fortissimo* at measure 170, leaving no room for the ultimate sonic climax in measure 176. As I often say to ensembles, "If you do not consider proportions and simply play loud, all you can do is let your eyes get bigger when the big moment comes."

There is a second climax that Camphouse refers to as the emotional climax, where a complete statement of the "We Shall Overcome" hymn is unveiled by solo horn. From my point of view, this stunning moment beginning in measure 187 must be uppermost in the conductor's musical focus as the work unfolds.

Then there is the matter of pacing dynamics to create an overlaying palette of sonic relationships intended to enhance the global architecture and artistry of a specific composition. This consideration goes far beyond the generic *fortissimo* is very loud and *pianissimo* is very soft.

By coincidence, as I was writing this chapter I was also preparing *October* by Eric Whitacre for a performance with the Austin Symphonic Band. It offers a compelling example of the need to consider dynamic proportion within the context of a singular piece.

October is comprised of 113 measures and is seven to eight minutes in length depending on tempo selection. Eighty-seven of those 113 measures have some kind of dynamic indication ranging from *pianissimo* to *fortissimo*. Markings of crescendo and decrescendo abound, and many are instrument or section specific as opposed to *tutti* dynamics. When I see this level of dynamic detail I am drawn to the conclusion, with relative certainty, that the composer has a very clear vision of his or her priorities for each line and for the relationships between various instruments and sections. Properly observed, the result is a constant and fluid fluctuation in color and timbre.

Equally, if not more, significant is the reality that there is not a *fortissimo* marking until measure 90 with the full forces of the ensemble at work. Then Whitacre calls for a second *fortissimo* on the lush G major chord at measure 104. Are these two *fortissimo* moments equal in volume? Or is there a hierarchy of dynamics that would lead us to conclude that the arrival point at measure 104 should perhaps be *fortissimo plus*, if you will? And if that is our conclusion, what must we do to pace the dynamics so there is never a sense of too much too soon? To me, these kinds of considerations all fall under the heading of proportion and are indispensable if one desires to make music at the highest level.

There is yet another issue of proportion that requires contemplation, that being the length of silence between movements of a multi-movement piece. On the one hand, we have the Holst *First Suite in E-flat*, where the composer specifically requests that the movements be performed with the briefest of pauses between movements to create a nearly seamless intertwining of the tightly unified material of each movement.

Another work where this approach might be appropriate is Symphony VI by Vincent Persichetti. To my mind, each movement should flow from one musical mood to the next. To my ear, too much of a pause between these movements seems to distract from the overall unity of the four movements.

However, other multi-movement works might call for a different approach. I submit *After a Gentle Rain* by Anthony Iannaccone, a two-movement work that is performed all too infrequently in my opinion. These two movements are contrasting in countless ways, yet the silence between the two movements tends to link them together into a unified musical gesture. The fermata in the final measure of the first movement is accompanied with the term *Lunga*, suggesting this measure should be dramatically elongated. This directive also suggests that the fermata should be followed by an equally extended silence prior to the contrasting, animated opening of the second movement. With this approach or interpretation, if you will, the two movements are unified as one, and the dramatic extended silence between the movements simply becomes a part of the music.

Then finally there are those multi-movement works that are, to a great extent, comprised of freestanding movements. Multi-movement compositions that fall under this category would include such examples as:

Four Scottish Dances	Arnold/Paynter
Scenes from "The Louvre"	Dello Joio
Suite Provençale	Van der Roost
Southern Harmony	Grantham
Suite of Old American Dances	Bennett
Suite Française	Milhaud

Most movements in these kinds of works can and often do stand alone. They are complete unto themselves. As such, I would propose that there should be a sufficient pause, a deliberate break in the action, between movements to allow the listener to reflect on what was just heard before the next movement begins to unfold.

This may be nothing more than a personal perspective, but sometimes I feel that one of the reasons we find the issue of proportion such a sizable challenge is the reality that we are creatures of technical, objective detail. We focus on what the composer has written, but while doing so we fail to take that next essential step to consider what the composer is saying. We obsess over every note, nitpick each rhythm, and methodically micromanage the mechanical elements of our music making. In doing so, we risk committing the sin of failing to take time to step back and contemplate the relationships and intertwining global aspects of the music.

If we accept that premise, it becomes a given that the notion of making proportion and/or relationships a musical priority will require a global perspective combined with thoughtful reflection. The musical truths hidden in the score are not necessarily revealed note by note or measure by measure. Therefore, considering musical proportion is core to our quest for artistic music making.

> There is no excellent beauty that hath not some strangeness in the proportion.
>
> — Francis Bacon

None of the above is to suggest that the end result we are seeking will necessarily be symmetrical. Symmetry and proportion are not one and the same. Certainly, proportion can exist to create symmetry, but it also can be used to highlight impactful moments, create surprise, or even distort or exaggerate relationships to achieve an artistic, pleasing, or provocative musical gesture. It is a pivotal element of music that must be reckoned with. It is the essence of the art that we create.

As stated by Ken Follett in the preamble for this chapter, "Proportion is the heart of beauty." To ignore that empirical and compelling reality is certainly a sin.

THE ARTIST TEACHER

I have come to believe that a great teacher is a great artist
and that there are as few as there are any other great artists.
Teaching might even be the greatest of the arts since
the medium is the human mind and spirit.
— John Steinbeck

L et me begin with a brief preamble. Much of what I'm about to share has already been said. To quote the words of André Gide, French author and winner of the Noble Prize in Literature, "Everything that needs to be said has already been said. But since no one was listening, everything must be said again." And, in this case, said by musicians, composers, educators, and artistic human beings whose collective vision and wisdom far exceed anything I might personally muster. Thus, I come to you as a messenger deeply immersed in reflection on all that I might share.

If you Google "artist teacher" or, in reverse order, "teacher artist," you will discover a broad array of dialogue having to do with the topic. An entry in the Oxford Research Encyclopedia of Education proclaims that "an artist-teacher is someone who creates art and supports the creative processes of learners."[21]

Reverse the two words, search again, and you will find that according to Lynda Monick-Isenberg, a teacher with the

Minneapolis College of Art and Design, such an educator is "a practicing professional artist/designer with the complementary skills of an educator, who can effectively engage a wide range of people in learning experiences in and through the arts."[22]

Yet another point of view suggests a new kind of educator/ artist who is uniquely prepared to evaluate the vision and content of arts education, music education in particular, as we experience it in the twenty-first century. The more you research, the more you realize there is not a concise definition for the terms and that, indeed, this career path appears to be multifaceted and evolving over time.

Eric Booth, editor of the *Teaching Artist Journal* and acclaimed author known for his work with arts education programs around the country, has what to me is perhaps the most salient definition as it might apply to our world. There is a thread throughout Booth's writings that suggests an artist teacher has the ability, gift, or skill, if you will, to bring people inside artistic experiences. What a beautiful concept! And, if you think about it, in general that is what artists in all genres do. They draw us into their world of artistry.

So, why is this so difficult? Cindy Foley, the Executive Deputy Director of Learning and Experiences at the Columbus Museum of Art, puts it this way. She believes unfortunately that arts education (insert the term "music education" if you will) has been impacted by the standards and testing culture like all other educational disciplines. Our focus has remained on teaching things that are concrete (translation: things that can be measured and tested). The bottom line, which is no surprise here, is that we teach to the test. In our world we focus on the elements we can measure, such as right notes, intonation, articulation, dynamics, rhythm, and tempo. The list goes on. And these are all viewed through an objective lens designed to focus on the "measurability" of each of these individual elements of music, resulting in an attempt to measure them against a predetermined, arbitrary scale or rubric that often contradicts or is in conflict with the very reason these essential musical elements exist.

Let's look at this notion from some different points of view. French horn aficionado Philip Farkas made a brilliant comparison between our obsession with every little objective detail of our music making and the actions of an art expert when he wrote,

> This is somewhat like the art expert who examines a painting up close with a magnifying glass. The expert can tell you that the artist was left-handed, used a palette knife, and had the light coming over his right shoulder. But when asked, "What is the subject of the painting?" the response is, "Oh, I forgot to notice!" Certainly, everything the art expert observed was correct, but it failed to embrace the single reason the painting exists in the first place, that being an outward expression of the painter's artistic intent.[23]

Henry Coward, British conductor and choral specialist, put it another but equally impactful way. In his book *Choral Technique and Interpretation*, he suggests that the conductor or performer can easily lose sight of the expressive qualities of the music at hand for any number of reasons. He states,

> This may arise not so much from lack of artistic perception as from his giving undue attention to some particular aspect or aspects of the work in hand—correctness of music, rigid regard to tempo, literal performance of the *p's* and *f's* of

the copy—so that it or they crowd out the poetic element of expression, and instead of his being an emotional artist he is merely a human metronome.[24]

In other words, he or she focuses on a mere obsession with the mechanics of the score. Whatever the rationale, the outcome is an objective mindset that fails to embrace the greater musical meaning or assimilate the comprehensive artistic content of the objective musical information that resides on the printed page. Now, read Coward's statement again and ask yourself the question, "Do you want to be an emotional artist or do you want to be a human metronome?" That book was written in 1914, by the way.

All of these narratives, to one degree or another, offer clear evidence of our music making shortcomings. We have allowed ourselves to focus on what I'm calling literal music making as opposed to the more noble pursuit of imaginative, artistic music making. In our desire to "get it correct" we have failed to "make it right."

> Mere 'correctness,' in fact, accomplishes very little.
>
> — Gunther Schuller in *The Compleat Conductor* (p. 15)

So how do we eliminate, or at least minimize, our music making transgressions? How do we commit fewer sins and begin to make the transition from our routine world of literal music making to a place where, as Eric Booth describes it, we bring students inside artistic experiences?

Let me propose the following initiatives and strategies for your consideration. It is my belief that a deliberate, creative application of these principles and practices to our world of music education has the potential to deepen our artistry and enhance the trajectory of what we bring to our students every day.

THE NECESSITY OF REFLECTION

The American philosopher and education visionary John Dewey told us that we do not learn from our experiences but rather from our reflection on our experiences. To put it another way, if you never take time to reflect on where you are and how you got there, it is unlikely you will ever be able to take yourself, and those you teach for that matter, any further.

Let me quickly state that this train of thought is not intended to suggest that we as music educators don't reflect on the craft of what we do. In fact, I would argue that there are few professions that do it better. We are forever examining our pedagogy, seeking new ways to deliver instruction, and expanding our rehearsal skills. Our educational conferences are filled with limitless sessions on new and better ways to teach—from starting beginners, to perfecting rhythmic precision, and elevating the performance skill level of our ensembles. We know how to do that. But is that enough and does it encompass all that is required to be an artist teacher? I think not.

To put this principle in context, pause to consider the meaning of the verb "to reflect." Multiple dictionary resources offer a plethora of applicable definitions, including but not limited to "the act of thinking deeply and with concerted focus." There are also references to the act of pondering, meditating, or unhurried consideration of something recalled to mind. Regardless of how you frame the act of reflection, there is overwhelming evidence that such exercises have great potential for meaningful, fruitful outcomes.

Jennifer Porter, a widely recognized leadership and executive coach, speaks specifically about "the conscious consideration and analysis of beliefs and actions for the purpose of learning." She goes on to say that "reflection gives the brain an opportunity to pause amidst the chaos, untangle and sort through observations and experiences, consider multiple possible interpretations, and create meaning."[25] Yes, her proposed strategies can become abstruse very quickly and sound like the stuff that haughty leadership conferences are made of, but pause for a moment to consider the potential benefits of reflecting on the musical outcomes, the art and beauty of what we do and how we share priceless components of music making with students.

Perhaps I should drill deeper and speak more specifically to the notion of self-reflection. To me that is not the same as contemplating "How did I teach today?" or "What did my students accomplish this week?" Instead, it's taking time to reflect on our musical core, the depth of our artistry, and our ability to infuse that artistry into our teaching.

So, what might that look like? In what ways might that go beyond what we already do? After all, we all listen to recordings of our rehearsals and "check the boxes" as we refine the mechanical content of the music we are preparing. We then compare recordings of multiple performances in an effort to identify our best work, almost always within the framework of technical mastery. But could we be listening for more?

In reality, our busy, task-oriented world is driven by the pace of our "doing." Music educators want to make things happen. It's in our DNA. One goal is achieved, and we are on to the next. A lesson plan is finalized, then implemented, and we immediately move to the task of developing the next one. A music cycle or concert is completed, and with little or no delay we are on to new music. The music we just performed is barely back in the library before we are in the midst of fresh challenges.

In so doing we miss a wonderful opportunity for artistic reflection—reflection of the highest echelon I might add. How often do we take the time to revisit, weeks or more later, the repertoire we have performed? How often do we listen not to see "how we did" but rather in terms of the artistry we achieved, the music we made, and what musical growth we and our students might have experienced?

I challenge you to set aside time to go back and listen to a particular work you have previously prepared and performed. Resist at all costs listening for the human errors that will inevitably be there. Also avoid thinking about Jonathan being such a nice kid and reflecting on how much he enjoyed playing his solo. For certain this is not the time to think about how hard you worked to master that tricky passage or perfect those complex rhythms. Those are all in the past. What remains is the artistry of the musical performance and the perceived impact it had on your students.

This is the time to hold yourself accountable for your sins. Focus on how the music unfolds, the nuance of the line (or lack of the same), how phrases relate, how the artistry of the piece is revealed. Ponder how sections of the ensemble interact and connect to create symmetry. Ask yourself questions such as: Are the dynamics compelling? Are the silences musically appropriate rather than sounding like arbitrary rests? How does the music emerge from and return to silence? Are tempo relationships proportional? Do moments of accelerando and ritardando unfold organically in a musically satisfying way? Is there a naturalness of expression? Does the music flow? Or does it sound more like connecting the dots or perhaps a sonic version of painting by numbers? In other words, focus on the music with the goal of listening artfully. We might call this "feelingful listening."

But, for us, this isn't always easy. In truth, from our teacher perspective we see notes, rhythms, and an objective landscape of concepts to teach and problems to solve. We tend to overlook those elements in the score that will reveal the artistry woven into the fabric of the music. My point is that a return to our music making in an inwardly reflective mode after the mission is accomplished has the potential to reveal to each one of us where we might be on our personal musical journey and help us contemplate what steps might come next to deepen our expressiveness and musicianship— the essence of being an artist teacher.

For what it's worth, it's been my experience that this kind of artistic reflection is best achieved listening *sans* score. Just sit back, close your eyes, and listen to the music.

THE DISTINCTION BETWEEN KNOWING AND FEELING

Let's begin with the notion that, in general, we find ourselves in this wonderful profession because of the way music made us feel. Of course, there were probably other factors, and for sure there was a teacher or teachers who "lit our fire" and then "fanned the flame." But regardless of the other influences, if we return to our roots, it was most likely that feeling that brought us to this juncture.

> I haven't understood a bar of music in my life, but I have felt it.
>
> — Igor Stravinsky

Then we quickly learned that to be successful music educators/ conductors who are dedicated to the educational growth of our students we have to know a lot in terms of craft and pedagogy. Those subsets of knowledge and skill remain central to our professional prowess, and we are driven to know more. But what is it that we want to know more about? What remains at the epicenter of our quest for ever-expanding knowledge?

Here is one answer. At the conclusion of a recent large state music educators conference, a survey was distributed to determine what session content future attendees would like to see on the program. Here are the results of that survey, including the percentage of responses supporting each topic area. Keep in mind that respondents could vote for as many topics as they wished.

- Rehearsal Techniques: 81%
- Instrumental Methods: 72%
- Recruitment/Retention: 56%
- Repertoire Selection: 37%
- Classroom Management: 36%
- Technology: 34%
- Teaching Methods: 33%
- Conducting Techniques: 32%
- Urban/Rural Challenges: 24%
- Philosophical Priorities of Making Music: 23%

As one can see, our quest for more knowledge tends to focus on the craft, management, and sustainability of what we do. Sadly, less than 25 percent of the respondents referenced music making as a priority. We see more evidence here of the previously stated premise that we are very preoccupied with and eager to refine the "doing" of our craft. This is not to suggest that these preferred topics are not important and noteworthy, but in our quest for knowing more, do we run the risk of feeling less?

Before attempting to answer that question, allow me to unequivocally state that it is not my intent to suggest that we don't feel deeply for our students or that we fail to have a love affair with our profession. Nothing could be further from the truth. From my travels and interactions with music educators and directors across this nation, I can assure you that our level of love and caring is second to none. It is clear that we feel for the activity of band and that the dedication we show for our students is boundless. Good on everyone! Now, it is the feeling for the art of music making as opposed to the activity of band that I challenge us to embrace.

First things first, let's come to grips with an understanding of the distinction between knowing and feeling. Knowing might be associated with the word "cognition," meaning the mental action or process of acquiring knowledge and understanding through thought, experience, and the senses. One can argue that the things we know are easily measurable. We can quantify our knowledge, compartmentalize it, and then access said knowledge when the need arises.

But *feeling* can mean a lot of different things in a lot of different contexts. Feelings can run the entire gamut of sensations, including but not limited to tactile or emotional awareness of some kind. The emotional landscape is limitless. So, for our purpose let's focus on a singular definition for the noun "feeling," that being "an emotional state or reaction." Specifically, in this case it's that heartfelt connection we discover and then associate with a piece of music. Without that feelingful connection all the knowing we can muster and all the pedagogy we call into play has little or no meaning or value. It is that "feel factor" that infuses the notes and rhythms with artistic richness and emotional outcomes. That is the world the artist teacher seeks.

It is my belief that students don't necessarily connect with what you know or say but rather with what they perceive you feel about the music you are collectively making. Let me give you an example. Saying "Trumpets, play louder because there is a *fortissimo* in your music" is a factual but feelingless statement. Try instead: "Trumpets, this is a glorious moment. Share your most beautiful tone quality. Your part is the high point of this moment in the music!" These kinds of student connections with the feeling inherent in the music are where the magic happens.

Let me digress and put this point of view in more pragmatic terms. A number of years ago I was listening to a National Public Radio interview with a country and western performing artist. He was at the apex of his career and was asked the question, "So every one of your songs seem to connect with people. You have one hit after another. Can you tell us your secret? How does that happen?" I will never forget his response, delivered with an earthy Southern drawl. He said, "I don't take on nothin' I can't feel." Point made!

Once again, knowing is important and an essential part of what we do. But it isn't enough. Feeling, a deep emotional connection with the music at hand, is critical if it is our intent to take our students to ever-deepening levels of artistry.

Robert Shaw was perhaps one of the greatest artist teachers of the twentieth century. We are indeed fortunate to be able to view videos of his magnificent rehearsals and performances. (Check out *Robert Shaw: Preparing a Masterpiece.*) He was meticulous in his insistence on the craft of the music, and his commitment to all that he knew about the music was ever-present. Nevertheless, what he knew about the music was always encapsulated in the framework of what he felt about the music. He often referenced what he called the "science and art of the rehearsal process." One must

> There is an art to not playing in tempo—an art which one has to learn, which one has to feel.
>
> — Pablo Casals, as quoted David Blum's *Casals and the Art of Interpretation* (p. 97)

always address both the science and the art of the music. Shaw's philosophy might be best recapitulated in the context of what we are discussing with these words. The *knowing* is the science of our music making, while the *feeling* is the art of our music making. They are both essential. When they intersect you are one step closer to your goal of being an artist teacher.

A THOUGHT ON QUALITY MUSIC FOR YOUNG BANDS

Now, one might say this all sounds good if one is engaged in the recreation and interpretation of universally proclaimed masterworks. But what about those of us who teach and make music in the world of Grade I–III repertoires? In response to that question I have some good news for you, and I have some bad news for you.

The good news? There is an ever-expanding treasure trove of outstanding artistic repertoire at the less challenging grade levels. More and more gifted composers are investing their creative energies in this noble cause. We are not talking about "educational music," but rather artistic music that is accessible to younger players. To my mind there is a significant difference.

The bad news? If your music, at whatever grade level, is not speaking to you artistically (translation: you are not "feeling it") then consider the possibility that you are introducing your students to the wrong music. Our goal is quality as opposed to quantity. Remember that you can only play one piece at a time, so always make sure that the music you select speaks to you and is among the very best that is out there.

EXPANDING AND DEEPENING ONE'S ARTISTRY

I personally find it fascinating that, regardless of the intellectual or artistic focus, one commonality is in evidence in all high-achieving professionals, that being a passion for growth. There is a burning desire, a hunger, if you will, to learn more, understand more, and feel more. There is that word "feeling" again. Let me share with you some examples from our musical world.

In 1956, on the eve of his eightieth birthday, the eminent German-born American conductor Bruno Walter was interviewed on National Public Radio. Part of the interview went like this. The interviewer asked the question, "Doctor, as you approach your eightieth birthday, in addition to your impressions of the past, what is your thought about the future?"

The maestro's response was as follows: "I do not consider what is coming for the future. I love to go on learning. I am perhaps I still to write something [*sic*]. Perhaps, if I'm allowed to still make music for some time. Whatever will come I accept it very willingly. I have full patience and full willingness to accept what life still will give, and I go on learning. That's all."

How inspirational! Here was a man nearing the end of his life's journey who had conducted every major orchestra in the world and collaborated with every major performing artist of his lifetime whose vision for the future was simply to go on learning. And I would submit that the word "growth" can easily be substituted for the word "learning" here.

There is an equally compelling narrative detailing a similar point of view expressed by the Hungarian-born British conductor and long-serving conductor of the Chicago Symphony Orchestra, Sir Georg Solti. Near the end of his book *Memoirs*, Solti, then in his eighties, shared an account of his plans to revisit and re-record selected masterworks from his past. His first step in doing so was to secure fresh unmarked scores to begin his preparation. In so many words, he stated he wanted to start fresh and look at the music through "new eyes." His closing comment on the topic was, "In my mid-eighties, I feel more strongly than ever that I have an endless amount of studying and thinking to do in order to become the musician I would like to be."

Both of these iconic conductors shared something akin to what is sometimes referred to as a growth mindset. Clearly their words demonstrate a love of learning and a desire to deepen themselves as human beings and musicians. Such a mindset gave them, and can give us, the potential and permission to allow our artistry to grow and evolve over the course of our lifetime.

Actually, most of what we are talking about here is simply growth. It's a no-brainer. Growth broadens us and deepens us. It sculpts who we will become tomorrow and shapes the potential of what we will be able to share with our students in the future. John C. Maxwell, author and organizational leadership authority repeatedly states, "Change is inevitable. Growth is optional." So true! Remind yourself constantly that we do not exist in a static world. We are surrounded by evolving stimuli.

> If you imagine less, less will be what you undoubtedly deserve.
>
> — Debbie Millman, American writer, educator, artist, curator, and designer

Change is all around us. It is present in every life experience and unquestionably imbedded in every piece of music we hear, study, teach, or perform. At every juncture in our lives we have the option to rush to embrace change or, tragically, to push it away.

What are some resources for deepening one's artistry? What experiences and thought processes afford us opportunities for growth? Look around you. The resources appear to be limitless.

After all, there is an extensive intellectual community of life coaches and motivational speakers who are prepared to share "the secret" of lifelong learning and self-improvement in one form or another. The library shelves are filled with volumes that address the topic from every perspective. Where does one even start?

For our purpose I propose we keep it simple. For me personally, regardless of the expansiveness, subtleness, or nuance of the topic, in our musical world these kinds of growth experiences can ultimately be traced back to two fundamental sources of inspiration. They are found in our interactions with other human beings or revealed through inspiring musical experiences that expand the breadth and depth of our existence. Let's look at some examples in no particular order of priority.

> A comfort zone is a beautiful place, but nothing ever grows there.
>
> — Author Unknown

THE RICHNESS OF HUMAN INTERACTION

First, at every opportunity spend time with smart people. I've heard it said that if you find you are the smartest person in the room it's time to check out another room. This notion can certainly sound egocentric, but there is wisdom here. Simply put, we grow when we elevate our environment and interact with people who challenge us intellectually and artistically.

But as we embark on this discussion let me quickly add that in truth there is nothing evil about being the smartest person in the room. In fact, it can be a good thing. Being "that person" affords one the opportunity to share one's passion, knowledge, and wisdom with others. You become the "teacher." In that role others are looking to you for who you are and what you have to offer. That is a role each of us must willingly and gladly accept. So, as we seek opportunities for our own personal growth, we must remain steadfast in our commitment to the act of sharing who we are and what we have to offer with other members of our profession. Never forget, we are all in this together.

The legendary golf teacher and author Harvey Penick is supposed to have said, "If you want to be a better golfer, don't have lunch with average players." However you frame it, it remains sage advice. Simply put, at every opportunity surround yourself with people who are smarter than you are, people who are immensely talented, and people who possess skill sets that are different from or more sophisticated than yours. Entering these environments is not always easy. It often requires that you step outside your comfort zone. But creating and embracing these opportunities can be a preamble to stimulating and challenging growth. You have to go for it!

In contrast, if you primarily spend all your time with like-minded colleagues, comfortably talking shop and reprocessing the status quo, these challenging and enriching experiences will forsake you.

Let me share a personal story with you. Some forty years ago I began a friendship with four professional colleagues that has been lasting and has deepened with each passing year. Today that friendship is one of my most priceless, cherished possessions. But in the beginning our musical and intellectual exchanges were an immense challenge for me. Many times when we were together in conversation I was speechless in terms of what I had to share. Their musicianship, breadth of professional knowledge, and general artistry far exceeded anything I had to offer. As a result, I would leave one of our encounters totally humbled by how little I knew about the greater musical world they all navigated so comfortably. I would return home with an overwhelming list of questions to research, books to read, and scores to study. Collectively, and to a great extent subconsciously, these gentlemen were expanding my professional horizons and deepening my artistry. While uncomfortable at first, these were priceless experiences that I treasure and mentally reference to this day.

Entrepreneur and motivational speaker Jim Rohn states that you are the average of the five people you spend the most time with. If true, then certainly the goal of interacting with bright, intelligent people who challenge who you are and who you are striving to become is essential.

Secondly, and perhaps an extension of the principle just stated, be prepared every day to meet someone who changes your life or redirects your focus, your vision of artistry, or your dreams. A little later in this chapter I will share such an encounter from my personal past. The year was 1986 and the person was composer Warren Benson.

Your awareness of and openness to benefit from these encounters is essential. As I begin the eighth decade of my life, I am eager to meet new people and interact with individuals who influence, inspire, and sculpt who I am

> Remember that life is a "do it yourself" project.

as an artist, teacher, and human being. Regardless of where you might be on life's journey, I challenge you to do the same. There is always room for shared human experiences that are mutually fulfilling and enriching.

THE QUEST FOR MUSICAL GROWTH

Broaden your musical plateau. Well, of course! But before we check this box let's view this reality from multiple perspectives.

Of course, experience and study music of diverse genres. That is a given. For sure do not shy away from music that makes you feel uncomfortable. Dig deeper. Listen to music that makes you ask the *why* questions or the *how* questions. To be honest, the first time I heard the Stravinsky Octet I didn't get it. I knew I should, but it just wasn't working for me. But over time and as my musicianship and artistry hopefully deepened, it became and to this day remains a priceless musical treasure for me.

Another tangent of listening I urge you to explore has to do with music that exists for multiple mediums, specifically, in this case, choral works that are transcribed for instrumental ensembles. It pains me to say this, but I can recall countless times I have worked with an instrumental ensemble preparing a piece such as *Sleep* by Eric Whitacre, the masterful Reynolds transcription of *O Magnum Mysterium* by Morten Lauridsen, or *Earth Song* by Frank Ticheli, and sadly learned that the director had not listened to or shared with students the original choral version or the text. In many cases the director had done some "homework," as they perceived it, by listening to a variety of band performances but had spent no time with the stunning original setting of those works. That's like looking at a black-and-white rendition of Monet's *Water Lilies* and saying, "I've seen them."

Here is yet another example. Personally, I have learned so much about phrasing from listening to great jazz stylists like (I'm showing my age here) Mel Tormé or Cleo Laine. I did not listen only for the entertainment factor or because I love jazz. Sometimes I would reflect on how they started or finished a note or where they added vibrato or subtly nuanced the dynamics, asking myself the question, "How did they do that?" Those were and continue to be growth moments for me. Those epiphanies have become a part of my musical palette and hopefully can be heard in my own music making.

Let me submit yet another kind of growth opportunity, that being to compare and contrast multiple professional level performances of the same piece, perhaps a major orchestral work such as a classic symphony, a Romantic tone poem, or something of equal scope. Of course band masterworks are viable options as well. Think big here! Now devise a strategy that affords you the opportunity to listen to multiple recordings performed by different ensembles and under different conductors. Now, as you listen begin to consider the uniqueness of each performance— the interpretation, if you will. As you do so begin to formulate judgments about what resonates with you in each of the renditions. I am confident that you will discover that you begin to listen differently. Your ears will become more "art focused" as opposed to "craft focused." It will deepen what you value when you hear great music played at the highest level of artistry. Why? Because the differences in the interpretations are where the art is.

Now, as you personally select repertoire, be mindful of the reality that in most cases the piece of music you select to share with your students is a part of a larger body of work. There are exceptions, but rarely is it the only piece by that specific composer. If for no other reason, this is why I encourage teachers and conductors to familiarize themselves with other works in the same genre by the same composer. For example, if you are studying, teaching, and performing *Sheltering Sky* by John Mackey, take time to become familiar with his other compositions, such as *This Cruel Moon*, the second movement of *Wine-Dark Sea*, or *Hymn to a Blue Hour*. I assure you that your artistic awareness of the music you are preparing will expand and deepen.

Finally, regardless of your depth of artistry, always, always be studying at least one work that is beyond your current musical plateau. If you perform mostly Grade II and Grade III music, I challenge you to own scores for masterworks such as the Hindemith *Symphony*, the Holst *Suites*, or Husa's *Music for Prague 1968*. Do not simply own those scores, but also study them. Furthermore, regardless of the level of music you are engaged with each day, I encourage you to routinely explore music from other genres, including but not limited to great orchestral works, choral repertoire, and chamber music. Doing so will exponentially expand your musical world and deepen the artistry you can bring to your students. Let me share a story I often tell.

I began my teaching career in Richardson, Texas. I vividly remember walking into the band office at Richardson High School when Howard Dunn was the director of bands. Howard was an amazing musician and teacher. Later in his life he was co-founder and first conductor of the Dallas Winds, first known as the Dallas Wind Symphony. His bands were exceptional. As I stood in his office I glanced at his desk and noticed a little pocket score of the Mozart "Gran Partita," *Serenade No. 10 in B-flat*. I wondered immediately why that particular score was there. To my naive, youthful eye it seemed out of place. After all, we were band directors. Why wasn't Howard studying his music for festival, a Broadway medley for his next concert, or perhaps other band repertoire he was considering for the future?

I must confess that I gave him a bit of a hard time about his choice of repertoire for study. I even posed the question, "Howard, why in the world are you spending time with that piece for twelve winds and string bass? You won't be playing that with your band." Howard answered, "I know I won't be playing the Mozart with my band, but I will be a better musician and teacher for my students in the future because of what I learn from studying this masterwork." This is the kind of growth I'm talking about.

THE MERITS OF THEFT

The notion of theft may seem a little out of place here, so let's start with a few quotes. Ernest Hemingway said, "In any art you're allowed to steal anything if you can make it better." Pablo Picasso boldly stated, "Art is theft." Japanese fashion designer Yohji Yamamoto asserted, "Start copying what you love. Copy copy copy copy. At the end of the copy you will find yourself." Igor Stravinsky proclaimed, "Lesser artists borrow; great artists steal." You get the idea.

Theft can be a good thing as it applies to the world of artistry. As artist teachers we should be ready, willing, and eager to steal, borrow, and imitate the world around us. It is yet another way to widen and deepen our artistry. And, as we do so, we then begin to put our own "spin" on what we acquire (steal) from others, and over time it becomes a part of who we are and what we do.

Let me be perfectly clear. The kind of theft we are talking about here must not be confused with the act of impersonating or pretending to be someone else. Attempting to do so simply defaces and destroys the unique qualities of who you actually are and who you might become. On the other hand, observing and emulating others' qualities and attributes in a tasteful blend with your unique assets and traits can lead to an enhanced version of who you are and who you will become. To do so is never a sin.

For extensive enlightenment on the topic of artistic theft, I highly recommend reading *Steal Like an Artist: 10 Things Nobody Told You About Being Creative* by Austin Kleon (Workman Publishing Company).

So, where do we go next? During our discussion of the richness of human interaction I promised you a story. To be honest, it is clearly one of those life-changing experiences in my personal life. It happened at a College Band Directors National Association Conference at the University of Kansas in January of 1986. One of the featured speakers was Warren Benson, professor of composition at the Eastman School of Music. One of his sessions carried the title "The Music of Warren Benson." In truth, the lecture went far beyond his music, offering profound insights into his vision, passion, and intellect. It was a transforming hour for me and one of those pivotal moments that challenged me to rethink some core beliefs about the artistry of what we do each day.

Benson went into great detail defining the relationship between himself, the composer, and us, the conductors and teachers. So much of what he had to say encapsulates much of what this book has attempted to convey.

He started with a description of how the process unfolds. It was his belief that the composer comes up with an idea, a vision, or perhaps a concept. Then he strives to define that idea, vision, or concept in the form of a new composition. He went on to suggest that it might be a timbral idea, a textural idea, a melodic idea, a structural issue, or a harmonic sequence—or a combination of musical attributes. As the process continues, the ideas come into shape, morphing into a sequence of musical symbols that he wants to share as music. The process of editing and defining brings clarity to the score. Then the score is done, and it hasn't made any noise.

He then hands the score to you, the conductor/teacher. You start with what you see: instrumentation, musical information, tempi, meters, dynamics, and so on. As you continue to examine the score, you begin to identify those elements and give them relevance. Obviously there is a phrase here! Here is another! More study and reflection identify relationships between phrases. You decide these phrases need to be connected seamlessly. Subtle dynamics intended to define and shape the phrases begin to take shape. And while there is simply a *mezzo piano* marking in the score, you decide there should be a little rise in the volume to strengthen the connections.

Harmonies begin to have relevance that suggests they should be highlighted or underscored. You then determine elements in the percussion trigger new entrances in the winds and that they should be emphasized to define that moment. The more you define these variables, the more you define how you want to do the piece, how you want it to go. And the more you know how you want the piece to go, the more you take possession of it. Then the more you take possession of it, the more you own it and the more it becomes yours. Your interpretation. How you feel about it.

Benson paused reflectively and then summarized, "And that is where the composer and the conductor/educator meet. Out there . . . where the composer feels about it and where you, the conductor/educator, feels about it." That confluence of feelings then becomes the catalyst for the artistry we all seek to share with our students. That is the world of the artist teacher. That is our ultimate destination.

Strive to be the teacher you would like to learn from
and
Strive to be the conductor you would like to play for.

ENDNOTES

1. Bruce Adolphe, *What to Listen for in the World* (New York: Limelight Editions, 1996), 76.
2. Ruth Waterman, "Writing," accessed May 5, 2020, https://ruthwaterman.com/writing/
3. Bruno Walter, as quoted in: David Blum, *Casals and the Art of Interpretation* (Los Angeles: University of California Press, 1980), p. 71
4. Pablo Casals, as quoted in: Josep Maria Corredor, *Conversations with Casals*, trans. André Mangeot (London: Hutchinson, 1956), 153.
5. Pablo Casals, as quoted in: Ibid., 182–183.
6. Pablo Casals, as quoted in: Blum, *Casals and the Art of Interpretation*, p. 63
7. Alfred Christlieb Kalischer and Ludwig van Beethoven, *Beethoven's Letters: A Critical Edition with Explanatory Notes*, trans. John South Shedlock (London: J. M. Dent, 1909), 101.
8. Pablo Casals, as quoted in: Blum, *Casals and the Art of Interpretation*, 15.
9. James Boyk, "Dynamic Inflection and the Beauty of Live Music," accessed May 6, 2020, https://www.cco.caltech.edu/~boyk/inflection.htm.
10. Bruno Walter, as quoted in: Blum, *Casals and the Art of Interpretation*, 71.
11. Bruno Walter, as quoted in: Ibid., 71.
12. Adolphe, *What to Listen for in the World*, 36.

13. Daniel Gregory Mason, "The Tyranny of the Bar-Line," *The New Music Review and Church Music Review* 9 (1909): 33.

14. Gunther Schuller, *The Compleat Conductor* (Oxford: Oxford University Press, 1997), 14.

15. David McGill, *Sound in Motion: A Performer's Guide to Greater Musical Expression* (Bloomington: Indiana University Press, 2007), 266.

16. Daniel Barenboim, *A Life in Music* (New York: Arcade Publishing, 2002), 53.

17. Boyk, "Dynamic Inflection and the Beauty of Live Music," accessed May 6, 2020.

18. Paul Hillier, *Arvo Pärt* (Oxford: Oxford University Press, 1997), 1.

19. Lesley Sisterhen McAllister, *The Balanced Musician: Integrating Mind and Body for Peak Performance* (United Kingdom: Scarecrow Press, 2013), 244.

20. Blum, *Casals and the Art of Interpretation*, 98.

21. Esther Sayers, "The Artist-Teacher," *Oxford Research Encyclopedias*, published March 2019, https://doi.org/10.1093/acrefore/9780190264093.013.401

22. Lynda Monick-Isenberg, as quoted in: Marcia LaCerte, "A Teaching Artist, Not an Art Teacher," accessed May 7, 2020, https://mcad.edu/features/teaching-artist-not-art-teacher.

23. Philip Farkas, *The Art of Musicianship* (Bloomington, IN: Musical Publications, 1976), 17.

24. Henry Coward, *Choral Technique and Interpretation* (New York: H. W. Gray, 1914), 90.

25. Jennifer Porter, "Why You Should Make Time for Self-Reflection (Even if You Hate Doing It)," accessed May 7, 2020, https://hbr.org/2017/03/why-you-should-make-time-for-self-reflection-even-if-you-hate-doing-it.

BIBLIOGRAPHY

Adolphe, Bruce. *What to Listen for in the World*. New York: Limelight Editions, 1996.

Barenboim, Daniel. *A Life in Music*. New York: Arcade Publishing, 2002.

Blum, David. *Casals and the Art of Interpretation*. Los Angeles: University of California Press, 1980.

Boyk, James. "Dynamic Inflection and the Beauty of Live Music." Accessed May 6, 2020. https://www.cco.caltech.edu/~boyk/inflection.htm.

Corredor, Josep Maria. *Conversations with Casals*. Translated by André Mangeot. London: Hutchinson, 1956.

Coward, Henry. *Choral Technique and Interpretation*. New York: H. W. Gray, 1914.

Farkas, Philip. *The Art of Musicianship*. Bloomington, IN: Musical Publications, 1976.

Hillier, Paul. *Arvo Pärt*. Oxford: Oxford University Press, 1997.

Kalischer, Alfred Christlieb, and Ludwig van Beethoven. *Beethoven's Letters: A Critical Edition with Explanatory Notes*. Translated by John South Shedlock. London: J. M. Dent, 1909.

LaCerte, Marcia. "A Teaching Artist, Not an Art Teacher." Accessed May 7, 2020. https://mcad.edu/features/teaching-artist-not-art-teacher.

Losseff, Nicky, and Jenny Doctor. *Silence, Music, Silent Music.* Hampshire, England: Ashgate Publishing, 2007.

Mason, Daniel Gregory. "The Tyranny of the Bar-Line." *The New Music Review and Church Music Review* 9 (1909): 33.

McAllister, Lesley Sisterhen. *The Balanced Musician: Integrating Mind and Body for Peak Performance.* United Kingdom: Scarecrow Press, 2013.

McGill, David. *Sound in Motion: A Performer's Guide to Greater Musical Expression.* Bloomington, IN: Indiana University Press, 2007.

Porter, Jennifer. "Why You Should Make Time for Self-Reflection (Even if You Hate Doing It)." Accessed May 7, 2020. https://hbr.org/2017/03/why-you-should-make-time-for-self-reflection-even-if-you-hate-doing-it.

Sayers, Esther. "The Artist-Teacher." *Oxford Research Encyclopedias.* Published March 2019. https://doi.org/10.1093/acrefore/9780190264093.013.401.

Schuller, Gunther. *The Compleat Conductor.* Oxford: Oxford University Press, 1997.

Waterman, Ruth. "Writing." Accessed May 5, 2020. https://ruthwaterman.com/writing/

ABOUT THE AUTHOR

Richard Floyd has enjoyed a distinguished career at virtually every level of wind band performance. He most recently retired as the University Interscholastic League State Director of Music at the University of Texas at Austin and now holds the title Texas State Director of Music Emeritus. He also serves as Musical Director and Conductor of the Austin Symphonic Band, viewed to be one of the premier adult concert bands in America.

Prior to his appointment at the University of Texas, Mr. Floyd served on the faculty at the University of South Florida and as director of bands at Baylor University, where he elevated the Baylor University Wind Ensemble to national prominence. He began his career as a middle school and high school band director in the famed Richardson Texas Public Schools.

His ensembles have performed at numerous state and national conventions and conferences, including the 1977 College Band Directors National Association, the 1981 Music Educators National Conference, and concerts at the Midwest International Clinic in Chicago in 1989, 1997, and 2007. Other distinguished performances include concerts for the American Bandmasters Association in 1993 and 2006 and the 2004 Western International Band Clinic in Seattle, Washington. In addition, he has toured extensively as a clinician, conductor, and lecturer throughout the United States and eleven other countries.

The Texas Bandmasters Association (TBA) named him Texas Bandmaster of the Year in 2006 and presented him with the TBA Lifetime Administrative Achievement Award in 2008. He received the Texas Music Educators Association Distinguished Service Award in 2009 and was inducted into the Bands of America Hall of Fame and Texas PBM Hall of Fame in 2011. In 2011 he was awarded the Midwest International Band and Orchestra Clinic Medal of Honor for distinguished service to the profession. In 2014 he was inducted into the National Band Association Academy of Wind and Percussion Arts and was also honored with the Kappa Kappa Phi Distinguished Service to Music medal. Most recently, in December of 2018, he was honored as a Midwest Clinic Legend in recognition of his lifetime contributions to music education.

Mr. Floyd held the post of National Secretary for the College Band Directors National Association from 1979 to 2007, and he has played an active leadership role in that organization's mission for over three decades. He currently serves on the board of directors for Music For All and is a Yamaha Master Educator.

In 2006 he was featured on the DVD *Kindred Spirits* from the series *Conducting from the Inside Out*, published by GIA Publications. Other conductors featured include H. Robert Reynolds, Craig Kirchhoff, and Allan McMurray. In 2015 his book *The Artistry of Teaching and Making Music* was published to critical acclaim by GIA Publications.

Paramount in his life is his wife Cheryl, who enjoys her own distinguished career as one of the premier middle school band directors in the nation.